Old Testament Studies

Rudolf Frieling was born in 1901 in Leipzig, Germany. He studied theology and philosophy and took his Ph.D. at Leipzig. He was among those who founded The Christian Community in 1922, and was its leader from 1960 until his death in 1986. Among his works are *Christianity and Reincarnation*, *Christianity and Islam*, and *Hidden Treasures in the Psalms* which are available from Floris Books.

Rudolf Frieling

Old Testament Studies

Essays

Trees, Wells, and Stones
in the Lives of the Patriarchs

From Sabbath to Sunday

Floris Books

The Essays were originally published in German under the title
Bibel-Studien by Verlag Urachhaus in 1963. Translated by
Margaret and Rudolf Koehler.

'Trees, Wells, and Stones in the Lives of the Patriarchs' was
originally published in German under the title *Von Bäumen,
Brunnen und Steinen in den Erzvätergeschichten* by Verlag
Urachhaus (third edition in 1963). Originally translated by
Alfred Heidenreich and published in English in *The Christian
Community* journal 1935. Revised and compared with latest
German edition for this publication.

'From Sabbath to Sunday' was originally published in German
under the title *Der Sonntag — eine christliche Tatsache* by Verlag
Urachhaus in 1965. Translated by Donald Maclean.

British Library Cataloguing in Publication Data

Frieling, Rudolf
Old Testament studies.
1. Bible. O.T.—Criticism, interpretation, etc.
I. Title II. Studien zum alten Testament. *English*
221.6   BS1171.2

ISBN 0-86315-057-8

Printed in Great Britain
by Billing & Son Ltd, Worcester

Contents

Acknowledgements

Unless otherwise stated, all quotations from the Bible are from the Revised Standard Version (RSV) with kind permission of the National Council of the Churches of Christ. (New Testament © 1946, 1971; Old Testament © 1952). Empasis in the quotations are the author's.

When the context has required the Authorised Version (AV) has sometimes been used, or the author's own translation.

ESSAYS ON THE OLD TESTAMENT

1. The creation of man in the first chapter of Genesis

The first page of the Bible describes the creation. 'In the beginning God created the heavens and the earth'. The world comes into being in the course of six days, man appearing on the last of them.

It is evident from the way it is told that man is not just the last in a series of creations but constitutes the final and crowning glory. As the supreme creation, therefore, he also has the potentiality of growing beyond mere 'createdness' and by virtue of his own being rising to become a fellow creator.

The style of the first chapter of Genesis emphasizes this special quality in man. Even a superficial glance shows that no other day of creation takes up so much space in this concise chapter, but the distinction can be observed in subtler details. We are well aware for example that the account of each day of creation ends with a particular phrase: 'And the evening and the morning were the first day . . . the second day . . .' as the Authorized Version has it. Closer study of the Hebrew shows that this almost liturgical, rhythmical repetition is not absolutely identical for the different days. The first day is not so called, but 'one' day: 'And there was evening and there was morning, one day' (RSV). An organic cycle of time has been formed as something separate and unique. It is only with the second day that the ordinal numbers appear, and even then we do not find 'the second day . . . the third day' but 'second day . . . third day'. This continues up to and including the fifth day. But then comes '*the* sixth day' (1:31). This is more emphatic. The seventh day has no concluding formula like the others but has instead the distinction of being called 'the seventh day' three times (2:2,3). The solemnity of the divine rest it comprises, however, is an indication of the uniqueness of the events of the sixth day.

On the other hand the sixth day is not wholly 'reserved' for man. You would think the 'day of man' would be more strikingly unique if it had no other content. But the sixth day begins with the bringing forth of the creatures of the firm land, the warm-blooded mammals. This comes very close to the creation of man — which is also in line with modern scientific views. Genesis, however, sees not only this closeness but at the same time the huge difference between man and animal. This comes out very clearly by virtue of the juxtaposition. The gradually advancing development of organic forms has come close to the human, but man's actual coming into existence occurs only as a result of the entry of a quite new element from above, which had to await this moment in evolution to make its impact.

Until now we read in each case that God said, 'Let there be . . .': 'Let there be light . . . Let there be a firmament . . .' or 'Let the waters . . . be gathered together . . . let the dry land appear.' It is quite different with man. A unique and most solemn prologue precedes his creation (Gen. 1:26).

1 The prologue

Then God said,
'Let us make man
in our image,
after our likeness;
and let them have dominion
over the fish of the sea,
and over the birds of the air,
and over the cattle,
and over all the earth,

and over every creeping thing
that creeps upon the earth.' (Gen.1:26).

The 'Let us . . .' is like an appeal of the divine soul to its own creative powers, which in their manifoldness are addressed in the plural and which, while within God, are yet beings in their own right. What is translated as 'God' is in the original *Elohim* — quite clearly plural. The related verb forms, however, are nearly always in the singular.★ *Elohim* is therefore a unified body of sublime beings through which God himself works. The prologue is unique in that here the Hebrew verb takes into account the plural quality of *Elohim*, and that this is followed by the plurals 'us' and 'our'. Three times the plurality of the divine soul utters itself: 'Let us . . . our image . . . our likeness'.

In this threefold utterance we receive, as if from the highest heaven, an intimation of the mystery of the Trinity in the Old Testament. Not only do the *Elohim* form the sevenfold entity of which ancient tradition speaks but, in still higher regions, the Trinity itself.

It is significant that such a highlighting of the 'three' occurs just here in connection with the creation of man, for it is only in relation to the number three that man's true nature can be understood. Simply as body and soul he would be no image of a triune God. He is spirit, soul and body.

The translation 'make man' is correct inasmuch as the original has only 'Adam', meaning 'man', with no article before it. In Hebrew this word indicates neither singular nor plural; it is like a collective noun.

'Let us . . .' Man has his origin in this great, divine first person plural. Then comes, 'in our image'. The Greek translation has *eikon*, the Latin, *imago* — the word used of Christ in a special sense in the New Testament. He is the 'image' of the invisible God (Col.1:15; 2Cor.4:4). The Son proceeding from the Father in eternity, who brings the

---

★See Chapter 2, 'God and gods'.

incomprehensible into manifestation, is the original image of all images. Man was created that he too might fulfil that image. He is one day to be raised to the likeness of the Son, changing 'from one degree of glory to another' (2Cor.3:18). Since man was created '*in* [literally] our image', then in him there also came into being the potential for what had been determined by the original image of the divine Son.

The 'image' springs as it were directly from the Father who brings forth the Son. The following introduction of the word 'likeness' (Greek *homoiosis*, Latin *similitudo*) presupposes the existence of intelligent beings who can comprehend such a likeness. Whoever recognizes the image that proceeded from the Father will find that it leads beyond itself as image, from the visible up to the invisible. 'No one has seen God.' But: 'He who has seen me has seen the Father.' So the 'likeness' touches on a motif of 'recognition' and anticipates the sphere of the Holy Spirit.★

This basic definition of 'image' and 'likeness' is connected with the prospect of the 'dominion' to which man is called. This raises him above all creatures and places him beside the creator as his earthly deputy, as one who may share in God's kingship. The living creatures of water, air and earth that are now mentioned represent different soul activities, and they reflect the whole complex of man's emotions. This complexity has to be held together in harmony at his own command, by his 'I'. The dominion God intended for man

★As an introduction to the genealogy from Adam to Noah the beginning of the fifth chapter of Genesis turns back once more to 1:26. The descent from father to son is thus linked with the creation of man and seen in the light of it. Of Adam (and only of him) it is said: 'he became the father of a son in his own likeness, after his image, and named him Seth' (5:3). 'Image' and 'likeness' have changed places, also 'in' and 'after'. Thus for all the similarity the difference from 1:26 is also meant to be indicated. The 'image' appears again for the last time after the Flood, where the death penalty is laid down for the shedding of human blood in view of the great dignity of man made in God's image (9:6). The two terms 'image' and 'likeness' occur only in 1:26 and in the repetition, 5:3, that reflects it.

over the animals is not merely part of a plan for the civilization of the earth; he is not only to cope with the animals outwardly and tame them. Great saints have been able to influence animals with ease since they had previously gained command over the animal within themselves. Thus to a certain extent we already anticipate the realm of the New Testament.

2 The act of creation

So God [Elohim] created man in his own image,
in the image of God he created him;
male and female he created them. (Gen.1:27).

Just as the 'we' occurs three times in the prologue, so here, where the transition of the divine thought into actual existence is concerned, the word *bara* (create), so rarely used in the Old Testament, also occurs three times.

In all, the word *bara* occurs seven times in the story of creation: Straight away at the opening: 'In the beginning God *created* the heavens and the earth' (1:1). Similarly at its close where the six days are finally summed up: 'God . . . rested on the seventh day from all his work which he *had done in creation*' (2:3), and 'These are the generations of the heavens and the earth when they were *created*' (2:4). So *bara* is used when the whole creation is reviewed. This expression should be distinguished from 'made'. God 'made' the firmament, the heavenly bodies and the beasts of the earth. He also said: 'Let us make man . . .'. But there is an exception with the first mention of ensouled life that begins to multiply in the waters and also took the form of the great sea monsters: 'So God *created* the great sea monsters' (1:21). And then in connection with man *bara* occurs in three consecutive sentences (1:27).

'Make' somehow presupposes an already existing substance out of which something can be made. The 'making' of man in the prologue takes place in the realm of divine thought out of which the creator forms his idea of man in his image. But now the thought is to take on its own existence, separate from the inner being of God, outside God. That there can actually be something that itself is not directly God is an immense and mysterious fact, one which philosophers have struggled to understand. Perhaps we can come closest to the mystery by means of the idea of love. To grant other beings outside himself their own separate existence God has as it were to delve into his own substance and release and give away something of himself. That is an act of love, a sacrifice. Wherever there is creation there is sacrifice.

There are two conflicting theological ideas: the one that the creation was a free, sovereign, divine deed, the other that it was an impersonal, spontaneous emanation. Apart from extreme views there need be no contradiction between a sovereign act and emanation. The latter should not, however, be thought of only as an inevitable natural occurrence, nor is it necessary to suppose that the creator is bound to disappear in his creation. But the idea — most clearly expressed in Islam — of no more than an omnipotent command, that cost the creator nothing, is too superficial. If we say for example that a creative artist has written his poetry with his 'heart's blood', should this idea not be true of the Godhead in a much higher degree? The poet's personality does not cease to exist; he has not lost himself in his poem. He has, rather, produced something from his innermost depths and transferred it to his creation.

In the 'Let us . . .' lies the free and sovereign resolve. But the *bara* that now actually produces man cannot be thought of except in the context of loving sacrifice.

'So God created [*bara*] man in his own image.' The second sentence seems to say exactly the same thing again: 'In the image of God he created him.' Even so it should make a profound impression on us; the pronouncement in the first sentence is so holy and so forceful that the text cannot easily proceed. But the repetition does not in fact say only the same thing again. The order of the words is different. The conclusion of the first sentence, ' . . . in his own image', becomes the opening of the second sentence. It is taken up again after a pause of reverent silence and now raised like a monstrance: 'In the image of God . . .' Behind this second of the three sentences there again stands the 'Son', the original image of all images.

The third sentence shows the duality of man's nature with the mention of 'male' and 'female'.* Genesis describes the actual separation into man and woman only after the story of the creation, in the second chapter — where Yahweh-Elohim puts Adam into a deep sleep and fashions Eve out of his rib (2:21). This division had therefore not come about till then. The apparent contradiction has been got over by supposing that two completely different creation stories were carelessly linked together by the 'editor' of Genesis. The argument is supported by differences of language between the two accounts (Gen. 1:1–2:4a, and 2:4b–25). It is quite thinkable that the two accounts resulted from the vision and literary formulation of different Hebraic schools. One need not exclude this possibility. The first chapter is concerned only with a supersensory, ethereal form of the world's existence, although it has already proceeded from God. The second chapter is more concerned with the world of matter. It is noteworthy that 1:1 speaks of 'the heavens and the earth' while this changes to 'the earth and the heavens' in 2:4b. The element of the dust of the earth is now imprinted upon the hitherto still ethereal being of man. The 'deep sleep' indicates a change of consciousness: he is asleep to the supersensory. Only now comes the division into sexes. Only now is mankind in the condition to meet the

*It is old traditional wisdom that mankind originally bore both sexes within him and that these only later separated. See abundant material on this in E. Benz, *Adam — Der Mythus des Urmenschen*. Rudolf Steiner has also corroborated this old tradition.

13

serpent. In fact the two chapters depict two different planes of existence. And if these were originally the concepts of different sages whose insights complemented one another, the 'editor' of Genesis was no naïve patchworker. Must he not deliberately have joined together the two accounts in the proper order as a result of comprehensive knowledge? Must it not have been clear to him that the original man, 'male and female', was not yet 'Adam and Eve'?

Yet the text reads: 'male and female he created *them*'. Scholars have expressed the opinion that an original 'him' has been changed to 'them' to eliminate the old idea as incompatible with Jewish tradition. This is not impossible, but such a conclusion is not even necessary. We saw that 'Adam' is a collective noun (p.9), and 'man' can also be one. In this prototypal realm singular and plural are not so rigidly distinguished; the one ethereal prototype holds many other possibilities. Thus the archetypal man appears as a unity when it is a question of his being the image of God. 'In the image of God he created *him*.' The third sentence throws light on another aspect of man's nature: the fact that he is also member of a human race. 'Male and female he created *them*.' The plural should still not here be taken as the duality of a man and a woman. At this point it is still the male-female within the one prototypal 'man' that shows its plural potentiality. Nor is the male-female polarity absolute even after the division into sexes; everyone still has the other pole within him, and is faced with the task of bringing about within himself the 'mystical marriage' in which the spirit and soul permeate each other. Marriage can be a more or less real image of that mystical marriage. But even those who do not marry need to seek this inner harmony, and by doing so will fit in more easily with their fellow men.

So the third sentence, which introduces the male-female as well as the plural motif, ultimately indicates a realm that belongs especially to the Holy Spirit, for it is the Holy Spirit that fosters inner harmony and the faculties for living in community. In the after-glow of the Whitsun experience it happened that the first Christian community, consisting of different kinds and conditions of people, both men and women, was 'of *one* heart and soul' (Acts 4:32).★

3 The blessing

After man is brought into existence through the act of creation (*bara*), he is given a special blessing as an additional spiritual endowment. A first blessing was already given to the animals: 'Be fruitful and multiply . . .' (Gen. 1:22). The fact that a living creature reproduces itself was felt to be the continuation of the miracle of creation. The blessing is an awarding of such real sharing in God's power that it remains henceforth with those blessed.

The same seems to be repeated for man: 'Be fruitful and multiply, and fill the earth . . .' (1:28), but it is introduced in a different way. In connection with the animals we read: 'And God blessed them, saying . . .' With man it is more explicit and more solemn: 'And God blessed them, and God said to them . . .' So far the creative speaking of God went out into the world, but he had no one in this world 'to whom' to speak. This is something entirely new. The blessing of the animals was not in a real sense spoken 'to them'.

The 'be fruitful and multiply' takes on a more profound meaning in relation to man, who is the image of God. As far as the animals are concerned it means a mere multiplication. Even this is marvellous enough, but what emerges are

★The beginning of the fifth chapter — already mentioned in the note on page 10 — once again looks back to the creation of man. There again *bara* occurs three times. 'This is the book of the generations of Adam [Man]. When God *created* man, he made him in the likeness of God. Male and female he *created* them, and he blessed them and named them Man when they were *created*' (5:1f). This is like an echo of the first chapter and only here is the giving of the name introduced. In the story of creation God named only day and night, the heavens, earth and sea.

always new samples of the same species. Man's biological fertility does not simply lead to a duplication of the parent. The species is the basis for the incorporation of new and unique individualities. Rudolf Steiner suggested that in comparing man with animals one should accord to the individual man the status of a species of his own if one regards his personality as something entirely his own. With man the mystery of singular and plural exists on a higher level, and the increasing of mankind is linked with the mystery of God's letting a host of invisible beings proceed from himself, 'the Father of spirits' as he is called in the Letter to the Hebrews (12:9).

So what is intended for man is not repetition of the same, but 'increase of the kingdom of God' by means of the development of different individualities incarnating on earth. Consciousness for those on earth in pre-Christian times was not yet fully awake. When in Old Testament times a man rejoiced in the blessing of children, his thoughts and feelings were chiefly concerned with the natural propagation of the species. The unrepeatable nature of the individuality was first brought to light by Christ. Therewith 'being fruitful and multiplying' also undergoes a profound spiritualization in that it becomes the concern of the inner life of the individual. The parable of the talents forcefully preaches God's high demands; he is not content for things to remain as they are, but expects an 'increase'. If man lets his lower self decrease and allows Christ to increase within him, then he becomes more than he was before. Then he becomes 'fruitful'. 'I am the true vine, and my Father is the vinedresser. Every branch of mine that bears no fruit, he takes away, and every branch that does bear fruit he prunes, that it may bear more fruit . . . He who abides in me, and I in him, he it is that bears much fruit . . .' (John 15:1f,5). What was intimated in Genesis here reaches its fulfilment.

From this point of view 'fill the earth' also becomes something different. For the animals, too, it does not just mean utilizing a space allotted for their physical existence. In every instance the animal is a divine and artistic component of the landscape, it belongs to it, completes it and 'fills' it, as a spring evening is filled by the song of a blackbird. Man, however, 'fills' the earth in a much higher sense. Anyone who has seen deserts or only recently civilized countries can all the better feel what it is to be on ground of an ancient culture where for centuries there has been spiritual striving in art and religion.

So although the words of blessing sound the same, they carry different overtones for man. The difference becomes even more obvious in what follows, where mankind is awarded something for which there is no parallel amongst the animals. 'Fill the earth and *subdue it*' — literally, 'put your foot upon it'. But physically taking possession, owning land, is still not the final goal. And the divine command certainly does not mean that man should blindly exploit an earth he has subdued by his techniques, and senselessly ruin its life. Again it is only the Gospel that finally shows what is meant. On the evening of the Last Supper Christ washes the feet of the disciples. One of the teachings that can inexhaustibly be drawn from that symbolic deed on Maundy Thursday is that man as a disciple of Christ should walk upon the earth in a different way from man bearing the mark of the Fall.

The blessing once more adds the motif of 'dominion' already contained in the prologue. There it shone out in the realm of divine intention, whilst here with the blessing it is actually awarded to man as a power: ' . . . and have dominion over the fish of the sea and over the birds of the air and over every living thing that moves ['creeps', literally*] upon the earth.' The same realms are named as in the prologue: water, air and earth — except that this time in relation to earth only the 'creeping' creatures are mentioned,

*The same Hebrew word is used as in the prologue.

not the 'cattle'. Perhaps this is already an oblique reference to the serpent, through which at the Fall man will lose his royal dignity.

4 The feeding

And God said, 'Behold, I have given you every plant yielding seed which is upon the face of all the earth, and every tree with seed in its fruit; you shall have them for food. And to every beast of the earth, and to every bird of the air, and to everything that creeps on the earth, everything that has the breath of life, I have given every green plant for food.' (Gen.1:29f).

From the Old Testament one hardly gets the impression that the ancient Hebrews were specially concerned about vegetarian food. All the more remarkable is the fact that Genesis first allows the eating of meat after the Flood (9:3). Here at the beginning plants are clearly the original human food.

Once again Man and animal seem to draw close to one another; there is the underlying necessity for them both to be fed. But again the differences are more telling. God turns first to men and speaks directly to them: 'Behold, I have given [to] you . . .' The word 'give' has so far been used only once in the account of creation when God 'gave' sun, moon and stars to the firmament, though translations obscure this. Now it is used with the dative case (the 'giving' case) in the second person; the direct address to man is even emphasized by repetition: 'I have given *you . . . to you* it shall be for meat' (AV. RSV does not bring out this second dative). In the following sentence the animals are not themselves addressed; food is allotted to them in the impersonal sentence: 'And to [them] . . . I have given every green plant for food.' How different in relation to man! The words directed to him begin with an appeal to consciousness: 'Behold.' The animals also have eyes but one cannot say to them, 'Behold!' Here for the first time in the Bible we meet this call to open the eyes and become aware. Man is not simply to go after his food instinctively like the animal. The taking of food is to lead the way to an act of higher religious perception. The animals also receive good things from God, but the response is missing — the lifting of the eyes in recognition, and acknowledgement of him in worship.

An anticipation of the great 'Take, eat . . .' of Maundy Thursday pervades the divine words in Genesis. At the Last Supper Christ gives the disciples his body and his blood in the Melchizedek meal of bread and wine, consisting entirely of plant substances, corn and fruit.

Daily nourishment is a basic fact of man's earthly existence, but everyday events can reveal the deepest mysteries. God rests in his own substance. The beings who have come from him, however, cannot exist out of themselves. From the divine Ground of the World there flows a continuous stream of life whereby everything in existence maintains itself. Thus on one occasion in the Psalms 'the bread of the angels' is spoken of (78:25). This experience of heavenly communion is reflected in man's eating and drinking, which is something between 'the bread of the angels' and the food of the animals, and can become either. In the one direction it can become the mediator of higher experiences. It can become sacramental. Eating and drinking does not thereby lose its reality and become a mere allegory, but opens to a higher reality and takes it in. 'For my flesh is food indeed, and my blood is drink indeed' (John 6:55). One could also translate: 'is the truth of eating, is the truth of drinking', is what earthly nourishment 'means'. The sacrament is more real than mere material food. The path leading to the sacrament starts with the grace before food, in which man begins to respond to the divine 'Behold, I have given you . . .' Without the upward glance human intake of food falls into the danger of sinking down to the animal level, where the image of heavenly communion is obscured.

Thus the creation of man on the sixth day is accomplished. Let us look back once more. First came the prologue, then the act (*bara*) itself, then the blessing, and finally the feeding.

The Christian Eucharist has always proceeded through four main stages: Gospel, Offertory, Transubstantiation, Communion. The renewed Eucharist of The Christian Community also takes this course; it is named the Act of Consecration of Man because the consecration for becoming a true human being in God's image can only be ours through union with Christ. Can the Act of Consecration of Man not open our eyes to the fact that the four holy stages also plainly appear in the creation of man, and correspond exactly?

The *prologue* in the creation story would then be the great *Gospel*, God's message about the nature and goal of man. Behind the threefold *bara* of the *act of creation* is hidden as we have seen the sacrifice, the *Offering*, of the creating Godhead, who brings man forth from his own depths and separates him from the Godhead for an independent existence. The *blessing*, which lives on in man as the power of increasing and being fruitful and of ruling the earth, confers the capacity for *Transformation*. This blessing is only fulfilled through Christ in the transformation of the individual man who 'bears much fruit', and the transformation of the earth entrusted to him. The *Communion* finally faces us in the fourth event where *God gives man food* for life in his plant kingdom — 'Take . . .'

2. God and gods

It is generally these days agreed in Christian circles that only heathens use the word 'God' in the plural. God is one. 'You shall have no other gods before me'. That settles the matter. Or does it?

It cannot escape a careful reader that the monotheistic Old Testament here and there mentions 'gods', and certainly not in a derogatory sense. Translations sometimes obscure this. If for example one consults the original text of Psalm 29, then it is not the 'heavenly beings' (RSV) but 'sons of gods' (*benē elim*) who are called upon. Similarly Job 38:7 does not speak of 'sons of God' but 'sons of the gods' who together with the morning stars 'shouted for joy' at the beginning of creation.

One is inclined to say that these are highly poetical passages; one does not take a poet all that literally if with artistic licence he falls back on certain obsolete forms of expression. On the other hand it is now time one knew that these old poets were not just whimsical storytellers. Other possibilities of consciousness and fields of experience were open to them which are for the present unattainable by modern man. The scholar Karl Kerényi speaks of the 'immediacy' with which the mythological pictures confront the soul. Slowly there comes a new understanding in this field, though the fundamental insights were already expressed by Rudolf Steiner half a century ago. The 'sons of the gods' were not products of the imagination; people saw them: superhuman beings shining with light.

The following passage from the Book of Job conveys an impression of how consciousness in ancient times actually still had other dimensions:

Oh, that I were as in the months of old,
*   as in the days when God watched over me;*
when his lamp shone upon my head,
*   and by his light I walked through darkness (29:2f).*

In those early times man's soul had not yet entered so fully into the bonds of his body as today; he still experienced his soul reaching out over his head and receiving the divine into it from above. Over his head still shone 'the lamp of God'. In a similar way Plutarch was still able to speak of the star of genius visible over a person's head.* On the other hand the actual sense world was still strange and hardly known, a 'darkness' through which man found his way thanks only to the light from above. Job still knows of such experiences from 'days of yore'.

It was by virtue of such facilities of vision that 'gods' were once spoken of. People had encounters with 'shining ones', and in whatever manifold and varying ways these radiant beings always conveyed the divine.

Finally, such an original experience of the divine through a host of higher beings is also indicated by the word mostly used in the Old Testament for 'God' — '*Elohim*'. That is undeniably plural. The singular is '*Eloah*', as for example in Job's 'lamp of God'. Otherwise it is almost always '*Elohim*'. It is an extraordinary fact that the word for 'God' in the monotheistic Old Testament is plural. On the other hand it should be noted that the verb to which '*Elohim*' is subject is not in the plural but the singular: *Elohim* 'creates', *Elohim* 'speaks', *Elohim* 'blesses'. At the time of recording this text, then, '*Elohim*' was felt to be a unity. Originally experienced as many, the *Elohim* had united in Yahweh, their head, and together formed a single spiritual organism, an 'Elohimity', as it were. Nevertheless, '*Elohim*' is originally plural and means 'gods'. One cannot avoid that. How is it compatible with monotheism?

*On the guardian Spirit of Socrates, Ch.22

For ancient religious experience the plenitude existing in the one God — 'the fullness of God' — (which also later came to light in the Christian conception of the Trinity) revealed itself through a manifold range of spiritual beings that God called into existence. The Nicene Creed speaks of 'all things visible' and also 'invisible'. People knew of the various choirs of angels, of the hierarchies up to cherubim and seraphim. The Letter to the Hebrews calls God 'the Father of spirits' (12:9). Within the realm of these hierarchies one would therefore also look for those beings originally experienced as the plural *Elohim*.

For the Bible such a rich and graduated world of spirits is an obvious fact. But, one may ask, is it therefore permissible to speak of 'gods'? Of highly exalted spirits, yes. But 'gods'? Supersensory experience is for the time remote from people of our age and they easily think in their abstract way that angelic realms are bound to obscure our view of the one God. They want to deal directly with God and not with the 'heavenly servants'. This shows that people no longer understand the word 'angel'. Angel (*angelos*) means 'messenger', someone therefore whose mission it is to establish a connection, a contact. God uses the angel as a delicate spiritual organizm through which he turns towards us. It would be foolish to refuse the proffered hand of a fellow human being because it is not the hand but the person we are interested in. The person himself approaches us through his hand; it is not an obstacle, but already serves to make contact. In the same way we may represent the relationship of the higher spirits to God — they serve him as his limbs as it were. If a spiritual being stands in the way and hides God from us instead of revealing him, then it is no true angel but an adversary of God; obscuring the view of God is the mark of devilish powers. The angels, however, are what their name implies. God shines through them — in various ways, of course, according to their rank. The eye of a fellow being speaks to me in a different way from his hand, but what it reveals is still the man himself.

So in ancient times a man could behold higher spiritual beings in great diversity, but what came to him through them was always, one way or another, God himself. This experience therefore naturally led them to be spoken of as 'gods'. These were still not — in the very first stage — 'other gods before me'. Not 'other gods' but fundamentally always the One in many forms. Indeed the old religions, too, had more or less of an inkling of this ultimate divine unity. It was only later that confusion and decline set in. The true gods were in many cases lost sight of and less pure and less exalted spiritual beings were able to take their place. The intrusion of demonic, even devilish, powers into religion is perhaps most clearly recognizable in the horrible cult of human sacrifice amongst the ancient Mexicans. If one takes into account this decline, this movement in various ways towards a twilight of the gods, one can understand why the gods of the heathens were so severely denounced in the Old Testament. In its final stages the old power of vision had become caught in the lower reaches of the invisible world, and finally faded out. It was his own individuality that the ancient Hebrew was supposed to feel called upon by the Yahweh-God. Grasping the idea of unity within his own being he was accordingly to be mindful of the ultimate unity of the divine, even at the cost of a certain abstractness. It is therefore no wonder that speaking of 'gods' became rare. The original plural signification of the word 'Elohim' was finally amost forgotten.

In one place, however, it persisted. In the Law of Moses the whole assembly of judges is spoken of (in the Hebrew) as 'the gods' (Exod. 21:6; 22:8,9 & 28). This is referred to in Psalm 82. There the unjust judges are presented with the fact that they have nevertheless been named by God, 'gods, sons of the Most High' — how serious therefore their failures! Behind this stands the conviction that a man should not actually judge and punish other men; higher beings must be called upon. The council of those pronouncing judgment was once such a closely knit group that it offered a temporary 'body' for higher beings to speak through. At such moments the men who judged were 'gods'.

In the same way the king can also be designated 'God' in the Old Testament. Psalm 45 celebrates a royal marriage and addresses the princely bridegroom as 'thou God' (original Hebrew 45:6). Is it oriental courtesy? It is, but that is no explanation. One must understand that such a courtly style, however empty and meaningless in its final stages, was in origin based on true experience. Once there were kings who were initiates through whom higher beings worked. The royal 'we' goes back to this. So the Psalm can address the royal bridegroom as *Elohim*. In the New Testament the Letter to the Hebrews quotes this passage (1:8f).

In the Old Testament the word *Elohim* can also be used for the dead. Saul goes to the 'witch' of Endor, who works with what we should call dubious occult methods, and makes her conjure forth the recently dead Samuel. It is not Saul but the witch who 'sees'. Saul asks: ' . . . what do you see?' She answers (literally): 'I see gods [*Elohim*] rising up.' 'What is his appearance?' 'An old man is coming up; and he is wrapped in a robe.' (1Sam.28:13f). These words describing Samuel as '*Elohim* rising up' have been allowed to remain in the Old Testament. Thanks to Rudolf Steiner's anthroposophy we can now begin to understand afresh such strange statements. Man incarnated on earth bears within and about him the lower kingdoms of nature — mineral, plant and animal. This all works into him from below. When he is excarnated at death, he is on the contrary drawn up into realms of higher beings. The angelic realms above him take him further and further into their higher existence; he does not cease to be himself, but he is permeated by their activities. It is possible to imagine that not long after his death a spiritual man like Samuel appears as it were in a

25

divine light, which in its radiance far surpasses what would be expected simply from his own being. The dead man, still recognizable by his own characteristics, already appears as if woven into a higher supersensory life. Since he shares in this divine life, he can himself be called 'God' according to those times, indeed even 'gods' — just as one uses the word 'manes' of the spirit of someone dead.

In relation to judges, kings and the dead there is an underlying original experience of 'sharing' in the divine. If one understands it rightly, it does not contradict monotheism. There is always basically the one God, but he gives participation in his divinity; he allows his divinity to be shared because in the depths of his being he is love. This first comes fully to light in the New Testament, and therefore we can find in John's Gospel Christ's words: ' . . . you are gods' (10:34). Christ quoted the above-mentioned Psalm (82:6) where God said to the judges: 'I say, "You are gods . . . ".' Christ recognizes as right the use of the expression 'gods' for men. He thus makes his own the promise which had been conveyed to men in a misleading sense from a quite different source, from Lucifer: ' . . . you will be like God'. This end can never be rightly achieved by following Lucifer. That can only lead to the God-likeness as a result of which men become afraid. One should not forget that it is Mephistopheles who makes this statement about becoming afraid,★ which seems so applicable today. But here, too, being afraid is of no use. Christ knows more than anyone about man's fallen nature, yet he does not make him afraid. Instead — by himself taking on humanity — he redeems the original intention of creation, that man should be the image of God. 'You, therefore, must be perfect, as your heavenly Father is perfect' (Matt. 5:48). In his technical ability, which rushes so far ahead of his moral ability, man today experiences that dubious God-likeness which can

★Goethe's *Faust I*, iv, 520.

indeed lead to fear. But salvation does not lie in going back, only in going forward — to where, through Christ, man can be led into his really true God-likeness. Christ confirms the saying, 'You are gods'. Potentially men are, though obviously the potentiality is not yet fully realized. Nevertheless, in his Second Letter, Peter can say that we may 'become partakers of the divine nature [*theia physis*]' (1:4), and in his First Letter (3:9), John speaks (literally) of the 'seed [*sperma*] of God' in those reborn in the spirit.

In view of the long distance that separates us from this great end it befits us to speak only with awed reticence about it. But the bold statement of Novalis is still a most profoundly Christian one: '*Gott will Götter*' — 'God intends gods'.

3. The sacrifice of Isaac

'He who did not spare his own Son but gave him up for us all . . .'(Rom. 8:32). Paul wants to bring home to the hearts of his readers what happened on Golgotha and makes use of a previously coined expression from Genesis. 'Did not spare his own Son . . .' These words appear in the unique account of the sacrifice of Isaac, in which Christianity has always seen a prophetic antecedent of the event of Golgotha.

The account is unique in its telling as well as its content and it is therefore worth examining in detail *how* the story is told.

> *After these things God tested Abraham, and said to him, 'Abraham!' And he said, 'Here am I.' He said, 'Take your son, your only son Isaac, whom you love, and go to the land of Moriah, and offer him there as a burnt offering upon one of the mountains of which I shall tell you.' (Gen. 22:1f).*

To begin with there is the meeting with the Divinity who calls the man by his name. He is thus called upon and awakened in the depths of his being. The answer of Abraham: 'Here am I' reads in the original: 'Behold — I.'

Now follows the behest. In the original text the name of Isaac does not appear so early as in the translation. First: 'Take your son'. One needs to have read the earlier history of Abraham in order to assess the significance of the birth of this son for the hundred-year-old man. The words that follow make us aware of the immeasurable depth of feeling that is bound up for Abraham with his son. 'Take your son, your only son, whom you love . . .' Then last of all is heard the name: 'Isaac'. The name encompasses in *one* word the whole world of feeling that has been evoked. And now comes the command to sacrifice him.

Here ends the first act. The impressiveness of the account lies in what is *not* said. There is not a word about what goes on in Abraham's soul: speechless terror, doubt, rebellion, resignation, as a modern writer would try psychologically to analyze it. Nothing at all. God's pronouncement simply stands there as higher reality, and as it stands thus in all its grandeur, the curtain falls on the first act. There is nothing to add.

The second act takes us on to the early morning. One can therefore assume that God's speaking to Abraham took place in the night, a time when the soul is more accessible to supersensory impressions. It is only the next day that reveals Abraham's answer. It is silently self-evident in what he does.

> *So Abraham rose early in the morning, saddled his ass, and took two of his young men with him, and his son Isaac; and he cut the wood for the burnt offering, and arose and went to the place of which God had told him.*

He 'rose early in the morning'. The first cold light of a new day can have a somewhat sobering effect. Not infrequently great resolutions, made perhaps without reservation in the heat of enthusiasm, are unable to withstand the effect of this dismal hour. Not so with Abraham. The truth of the commanding voice of God does not lose the force of its reality by passing over into everyday consciousness; it acts directly. Without a word and as a matter of course Abraham sets about bringing into effect on earth what he had heard in a higher world. Saddling the ass and hewing wood were prosaic morning activities. In the middle of the complex sentence stands the name, Isaac, immediately before the mention of the wood for the burnt offering. Isaac — burnt offering: we have to get used to associating one with the other. Has it really to be?

Thus ends the second act as tersely as the first. The ensuing interval is taken up by the journey.

Then with the words, 'On the third day . . .' the third

act begins. It is like a mysterious echo; the account of the marriage at Cana in St John's Gospel begins in the same way. It is not only a factual statement of time; one feels that it introduces something of a decisive nature, this 'third day'.

> *On the third day Abraham lifted up his eyes and saw the place afar off.*

It is as if he had journeyed the whole time with bowed head. Now he lifts up his eyes. In the Bible's mode of expression this lifting of the eyes always also has something of the sense of entering a visionary state. Abraham looks up and knows the mountain — the mountain that God had said he would make known to Abraham. This 'making known' has obviously now happened. It is the Mount Moriah which was later to bear Solomon's Temple. Looked at more sensitively one mountain is not the same as another; there is also something like an etheric geography, especially with holy places. The Hebrew *maqom* (place) is a significant word. It is used for an earthly spot where it was felt that the supersensory was invisibly suspended over it.

Abraham sees the place 'afar off'. It is possible for a person to experience something like a prophetic premonition if he sees from a distance a spot where something important will happen to him.

The great decision draws nearer. Already the 'place' has appeared on the horizon. A last stretch has now to be covered. This last stretch is momentous — even more so than the silent journey up till now. A decision is made: the young men have to remain behind with the ass. The ascent of the mountain is reserved for those making the sacrifice. The action moves on to an inner plane.

> *Then Abraham said to his young men, 'Stay here with the ass; I and the lad will go yonder and worship, and come again to you.'*

It is the first time in the story after his 'Here am I' that we hear Abraham speak. He cannot bring himself to utter what is to happen. He speaks only of worshipping and coming back. The inexorable determination to carry out the deed lies deep within him, but otherwise his feelings cannot yet keep pace with it; he cannot yet state as a fact that after what happens up there on the mountain it will not be 'we' that come back, but only a solitary 'I'.

> *And Abraham took the wood of the burnt offering, and laid it on Isaac his son; and he took in his hand the fire and the knife.*

It has often been remarked by commentators what an illogical love it shows that the father himself carries the knife and the fire lest the boy should cut or burn himself, when before long the knife will indeed be his death and the flame burn the tender body to ashes.

The journeying on together is interrupted by a short dialogue. But this is not an exchange of words that makes the going easier to the feelings of the two; it makes it still more difficult. It is part of the great artistry of this description that the sentence, 'So they went both of them together', is repeated in exactly the same words after the dialogue (verses 6 & 8).

> *So they went both of them together. And Isaac said to his father Abraham, 'My father!' And he said, 'Here am I, my son.' He said, 'Behold, the fire and the wood; but where is the lamb for a burnt offering?' And he said, 'God will provide himself the lamb for a burnt offering, my son.' So they went both of them together.*

The boy feels the burden of the silence. It comes as a shock to find him breaking it, but he can bear it no longer. With the divining soul of a child he senses something uncanny. His question goes right to the heart of the matter, but it is precisely the subject of the sacrificial offering that should not be mentioned. It increases the father's anguish immeasurably. The answer is evasive and yet at the same time unconsciously prophetic.

Finally, after the interrupted silence has again enveloped the two, the place is reached and the activity of preparation begins — without a word, in silence.

> *When they came to the place of which God had told him,*
> *Abraham built an altar there, and laid the wood in order, and*
> *bound Isaac his son, and laid him on the altar, upon the wood.*
> *Then Abraham put forth his hand, and took the knife to slay*
> *his son.*

Were it possible at first to feel the arrival and the start of the normal preparations almost as a temporary relief after the painful journey, then certainly a new tension arises now, the most intense in the story, which in those times must almost have torn the hearts of those who listened with every fibre of their being. It is brought about by the dramatic, inexorable sequence of the six verbs: he 'built . . . and laid . . . and bound . . . and laid . . . put forth . . . and took the knife'.

Then — literally at the very last moment — intervention and deliverance from above:

> *But the angel of the LORD called to him from heaven, and*
> *said, 'Abraham, Abraham!' And he said, 'Here am I.' He*
> *said, 'Do not lay your hand on the lad or do anything to him;*
> *for now I know that you fear God, seeing you have not*
> *withheld your son, your only son, from me.' And Abraham*
> *lifted up his eyes and looked, and behold, behind him was a*
> *ram . . .*

Twice the angel calls Abraham's name. When God himself at the beginning of the story spoke to him, he spoke his name only once. The ministering angel does not have the all-seeing, universal calm of God. It is as if he were drawn into the excitement of the critical moment, almost, one might say, as if he feared he might be too late. 'Abraham, Abraham!'

He who is called lowers the upraised knife and speaks: 'Here am I.' For the third time we hear this expression from his lips. The first time was when God called him, the second time when Isaac broke the oppressive silence, and now here in the last decisive moment. 'Behold — I.' There is a calmness about this recurrence. One is reminded of the words with which Goethe once characterized Abraham: 'Calm and greatness'. This calm and greatness, which enables him three times to say 'Here am I', has its roots in his solidarity with God.

In its austere beauty the account of the sacrificial journey to Moriah is a classic document of true religion in its earliest stage.★

★In this chapter we have restricted ourselves to the 'how' of the narrative. For what concerns the content — how the enigmatic event may be understood — we refer to the account by Emil Bock in his *Genesis*, pp. 123–41.

4. The building of the tabernacle and the creation

No true cult is the arbitrary creation of man; it has its origin in divine revelation. So, too, the building of the Old Testament sanctuary, the *tabernacle*, stems from the divine instruction imparted to Moses on the holy Mount Sinai. There the heavenly archetypes for the cult were 'shown' to him by the Deity himself. 'And see that you make them after the pattern for them, which is being shown you on the mountain' (Exod. 25:40, also 26:30 and 27:8).

The concluding chapters of Exodus (39 and 40) describe how what has been 'shown' finds its way into earthly reality, how the archetypes revealed 'on the mountain' take on material form and become visible to human eyes. Here occurs in little what happened on a vast scale at the *creation of the world*.

The biblical text indicates this connection very clearly. Expressions appear that are strikingly similar to certain words in the creation story in Genesis.

'Thus all the work of the tabernacle of the tent of meeting was finished' (Exod. 39:32); 'And Moses saw all the work, and behold, they had done it; as the LORD had commanded, so had they done it. And Moses blessed them' (39:43); 'So Moses finished the work' (40:33).

One can hardly read these words without remembering Genesis: 'Thus the heavens and the earth were finished, and all the host of them' (2:1); 'And God saw everything that he had made, and behold, it was very good' (1:31); 'And on the seventh day God finished his work which he had done' (2:2).

There is no doubt that this similarity puts the erection of

the tabernacle in line with the creation of the world itself. The outer world, then, is the great tabernacle, the macrocosmic temple, while the place of the cult reflects in little this divinely ordered world. Both worlds, however, reveal the eternal, supersensory archetypes.

It is possible to trace the correspondence of the two stories in greater detail. Like the creation of the world the building of the tabernacle is *a work of seven parts*. And this sevenfold nature of the work is made all the clearer by the use of the same expression seven times. It reads characteristically: 'As the LORD had commanded Moses'.*(Exod.40:19,21,23,25, 27,29,32.) It emphasizes that what enters the visible world corresponds with the archetype and that according to the divine will it is a worthy copy on earth of what exists in heaven. This echoes the expression in Genesis: 'And God saw that it was good.'

The sevenfold division also applies to the making of the priestly vestments;† there, too, is reflected the creation of the world, which Goethe calls 'the living garment of God'. However, we shall restrict ourselves here to the building of the tabernacle, where the relation of the seven stages of the building to the seven days of the creation is clearly discernible.

1

And in the first month in the second year, on the first day of the month, the tabernacle was erected. Moses erected the tabernacle; he laid its bases, and set up its frames, and put in its poles, and raised up its pillars; and he spread the tent over the tabernacle, and put the covering of the tent over it, as the LORD had commanded Moses. (Exod.40:17–19).

*Seven times, though not coinciding with the seven days: Gen. 1:4,10, 12,18,21,25,31.

†Seven times 'as the LORD commanded Moses' (Exod.39:1,5,7,21, 26,29,31).

On the first day of creation '*the heavens and the earth*' come into being as a first great 'above' and 'below'. This is reflected in the microcosm of the building of the tabernacle. The pillars rest on the firm ground and hold the tent-roofing aloft. What is stretched over as a roof, sheltering and enclosing, is in its cultic meaning the heavenly 'above', the tent of heaven.

2

The next stage in the building of the tabernacle is the separating off by a *curtain* of the *Holy of Holies*. In what could be called this 'occult' space, hidden from sight, is placed the ark with the mercy seat over which the two cherubim spread their wings: the place of the presence of God (Exod. 40:20f).

On the second day of creation God makes a 'firmament' in heaven and *separates the waters* above the firmament from those below it. Rudolf Steiner has pointed out that we should not envisage this 'firmament' as something material but as an area of supersensory controlling power, like a watershed, on one side of which the water falls down in dense, heavy drops, on the other side of which it floats as cloud in the realm of light and lightness, in the divine sphere borne by the cherubim. In ancient times it was a fundamental human experience that the upper world of clouds instilled a special sense of the working of divine powers.

This 'watershed', discharging water below it into the world of gravity and letting it rise above it into the realm of levity and light and mysterious heavenly powers, is pictured by the curtain which divides off the Holy of Holies, in whose secret place he who rules the cherubim is enthroned.

3

In front of the curtain, on the north side, is set up the table with the bread, (to the right of those entering since the Holy of Holies, in contrast to the Christian altar, was in the west, not the east).

On the third day of creation firm land emerges for the first time from the surging waters. Dry land and water are separated, and the land which appears is immediately covered with green *plants.* 'Let the earth put forth vegetation.'

This vegetation springing from the earth is then given to men for food. The earth becomes 'the table of the Lord'. On the Communion table there is bread and wine, the noble emissaries from the plant kingdom which as the body and blood of Christ are to become the food for eternal life.

This *table with the shewbread* is both a harbinger of the Communion table and a recollection of the third day of creation.

4

The fourth day of creation does not further the development of the earth since it is concentrated on the heavenly spaces. God creates *the heavens' 'lights'* — sun, moon and stars.

The cultic symbolism is wonderfully transparent in the fourth stage of the building:

> *And he put the lampstand in the tent of meeting, opposite the table on the south side of the tabernacle, and set up* the lamps *before the* LORD; *as the* LORD *had commanded Moses (Exod.40:24f).*
>
> *The table with the holy bread is the true image of the earth, the lampstand with the seven lights,* ⋆ *the image of the heavenly luminaries.*

⋆For the sevenfold lighting see Exod. 37:23.

5

After heaven's lights have appeared, life-bearing plants are followed by soul-bearing living creatures on the fifth day of creation. A *life of feeling* stirs in the waters and moves in the air. 'Let the waters bring forth swarms of living creatures, and let birds fly above the earth across the firmament of the heavens' (Gen. 1:20).

In these creatures the soul-element makes its first entry into the world. Essentially it is a stranger on earth. Its home is the heavenly world, which is why calling it 'astral' (*astra*, Latin for the stars) is fully justified. Man's soul is still kept back in the heavenly world which manifested itself in sun, moon and stars on the fourth day. He is to descend into the earthly only on the sixth day; on the fifth he still rests 'unspoken' with the Deity. The animal kingdom, however, already takes on existence before man. Its doing so is like a great prelude for the life of soul that will later be in man on earth.

This stirring, moving animal world of the fifth day, which has its being in travail and storm, in wave and flood, is a true image of 'astrality'. Such sensitive, freely moving phenomena intimate to us the subtle realm of the soul's activities.

Now mankind is called upon to transform the whole world of inner activities and desires symbolized in these animal forms, and so far spiritualize it that all his soul life is at the service of higher worlds. All inner activity is then suffused with a mood of devoted self-sacrifice. The symbol worthy of this mood of soul has always been the ascending smoke of fragrant *incense*.

In the cult of the Old Testament the incense offering was made every morning and every evening so that again and again the soul's aim was clearly set before it. 'Let my prayer be counted as incense before thee, and the lifting up of my hands as an evening sacrifice!' (Ps. 141:2) — words of which

we are also reminded in the Offertory of the Act of Consecration of Man.

There was a special altar for the incense offering. Its
setting up constitutes the fifth stage in the building.

*And he put the golden altar in the tent of meeting before the
veil, and burnt fragrant incense upon it; as the LORD had
commanded Moses (Exod.40:26f).*

6

The sixth day of creation then proceeds with the creation of
land animals and finally *man*.

Corresponding with this in the building of the tabernacle
is the erection of *the altar for burnt offerings*.

This altar for burnt offerings is bound to make an even
deeper impression than the golden altar for the offering of
incense. On it flowed the blood of the vicariously sacrificed
animals, the blood of the very warm-blooded creatures
closest to man that appeared on earth just before him on the
sixth day. In the blood of the sacrificial animals flowing
there he experienced the sacrificial offering of his own blood
to the divine world. In the burning of the animals he sensed
the consuming of his earthly being by the intensity of divine
fire.

In blood and fire are indicated the deepest mysteries of
the human being. In a way different from that of ancient
times, more spiritual but not less real, they are brought
home to us in every Act of Consecration of Man in the
closing words of the Offertory about the divine 'fire of
love', and in the mystery of the chalice. The altar of the Act
of Consecration of Man unites what was separate in the Old
Testament cult. It is the table with the consecrated bread, it
bears the seven lights, it is the place where the incense is
brought and, finally, it is the altar of burnt offering where
the sacrifice of Golgotha and man's own offering of himself
should meet.

There is a solemn significance in this correspondence of the creation of man on the sixth day and the altar of burnt offering.

7

The day of man's appearance brings the work of creation outwardly to an end. The seventh day adds no new phenomena, but it enriches the world inwardly with the element of hallowed rest.

God rests, God 'has a holy-day'. It is as if the divine lives within its own unique mystery, as if the Spirit were immersed in the depths of its own spirituality.

One should not think of the word 'rest' negatively as if it were synonymous with 'no work'. Not working outwardly should release forces that can then turn inward with full strength. It is also worth remembering here Nietzsche's saying about freedom, that it is not so much a question of 'free *from* what' as 'free *for* what'. A 'day of rest' epitomizes for many people today a sort of clean and joyless boredom. But the hands which rest from work are clean of the dust of working days, so that activity on a higher, divine plane is possible.

In the account of the making of the holy vestments there comes seventh and last the description of the holy crown with the 'plate . . . of pure gold' engraved with the words, 'Holy to the LORD' (Exod. 39:30). The seventh stage of the building of the tabernacle is also designed with this same idea of purification and consecration:

> *And he set the laver between the tent of meeting and the altar, and put water in it for washing, with which Moses and Aaron and his sons washed their hands and their feet; when they went into the tent of meeting, and when they approached the altar, they washed; as the LORD commanded Moses (Exod. 40:30–32).*

5. Balaam

1 *The king's messengers*

It was more than a thousand years before the wise men who beheld the star journeyed from the east. The people of Israel had pitched their tents near the Promised Land and were encamped opposite Jericho like a lion ready to spring.

Balak, king of the Moabites, knew that armed resistance would be hopeless. He may have sensed something of the spiritual force at work in this remarkable people who had crushed all opponents on their way out of Egypt, and whose camp fires now burned on the banks of the Jordan. In this situation the sword was useless to check the irresistible advance. In this situation, Balak felt, only a different kind of weapon would serve; a spiritual sword, the magic word from the mouth of one who had the full powers of blessing and cursing. Spirit would have to be opposed by spirit. He therefore sent his elders to Balaam far away in the east.

The seer dwelt on the banks of the Euphrates. The mighty currents and movements of this broad mass of flowing water, the gentle dulling of the physical senses by its roaring and rushing, the calling up of inner vision by the magical play of the waves — all helped him to attain other states of consciousness. While he was deep in prayer, the spirit gathered up his soul from his body, carried it to higher realms, showed it hidden things, gave it words of magic power. 'So Balak . . . sent messengers to Balaam the son of Beor at Pethor, which is near the River . . .' (Num. 22:4f).

He is to hold back this uncanny people with the sword of

his powerful word: 'for I know that he whom you bless is blessed, and he whom you curse is cursed' (Num. 22:6).

But Balaam cannot give an answer immediately. In bright daylight the inner voice is silent. He has to wait for night with its invisible flow, and in the silence of the night God's voice speaks. He should not go with them, nor curse the people of Israel, for they are blessed.

King Balak sends a second embassage, and offers great honour and reward. Again the secret revelation of the night has to be awaited. This time the voice allows him to make the journey, but 'only what I bid you that shall you do' (22:20).

2 Balaam's ass

In the morning Balaam saddles his ass and sets off. On the way he has a singular experience which is veiled in the fable-like account of the talking ass.

Balaam is making the journey in order to use the sword of his magic word. He should feel the immense responsibility. He should feel how fatally this sword threatens anyone who does not use it in pious obedience. A warning is given him. The reproving angel steps into his path and shows him the naked sword.

Balaam the seer does not see, but the ass does. One should read the biblical account itself (Num. 22:21–35) to feel its magic and appreciate the oriental narrative art — how it builds up — how the reproving angel three times stands in the road till finally there is no way of avoiding him and the ass sinks to its knees — how Balaam three times beats it, having no idea why it goes off the path, why it kneels down. Then 'the LORD opened the mouth of the ass'.

The suffering dumb animal, which nevertheless knows a great the man has no notion of, is for once finally permitted to speak — if we do not take this speaking too literally but more imaginatively, as a visionary experience of the prophet. The creature is permitted to open its mouth to answer the man who lays about it so uncomprehendingly.

But it does not indulge in violent accusation, furious protest, noisy lamentation. It remains quite humiliatingly matter-of-fact, and hits the nail on the head. 'What have I done to you, that you have struck me these three times?' The rider, however, responds with fury, even wishes he had a sword to kill the animal he thinks is mocking him. He has no idea how fatally close is the threat of the flaming sword from which the ass has saved him! But once more the creature speaks, immovable in its impartial matter-of-factness. ' "Am I not your ass, upon which you have ridden all your life long to this day? Was I ever accustomed to do so to you?" And he said, "No." ' How subdued is this 'No' after the previous thunderous outburst when he wanted to kill it! His rage has died down so that the eyes of his soul can now be opened to the angel with the sword.

The story has yet another aspect. The ass was also always the symbol of man's physical nature, whose task it is to carry his higher nature on earth. St Francis called his body 'Brother Ass'. The prophet Zechariah foretells that the Messiah will come riding on an ass, meaning that he would descend into the realm of earthly corporality. Christ entered the holy city riding on an ass.

Balaam the seer does not see the ass because he is riding it. He is not on the river bank, nor wrapped in the mystery of night, but in an ordinary state of daytime consciousness, and his visionary power fails. It is because his visions are usually only a result of a dimming of normal consciousness that his clairvoyance is a danger to the people of Israel, for whom the prerequisite for the coming of Christ is wide-awake, clear ego-consciousness. But now the admonitory apparition of the sword-bearing angel comes flaming into his full daylight consciousness.

3 The seven altars

Warned by the vision of the heavenly sword Balaam arrives in the land of the Moabites, where the king receives him royally.

The next morning he takes the seer up to the high place of Baal, to a holy mountain, that is, whence he sees the people of Israel encamped. Like the rushing river, like the silent night, this bare mountain height removed from the everyday world favours prophecy. However, a special sacrificial offering is still necessary to enable the magic word to be received and pronounced.

Balaam orders seven altars to be erected up there and a bull and a ram to be sacrificed on each of them. Animal sacrifice in ancient times was certainly not the butchery today's 'enlightened' arrogance often considers it. There was once a very vivid awareness amongst people that every physical phenomenon corresponded to something within themselves, that in each animal a condition or quality of the human soul was made manifest. The animal really provided an offering in a double sense: the man who brought it to the altar at the same time also dedicated with it to the deity the attribute of his soul represented by the animal.

Bulls and rams are sacrificed on the seven altars. These altars are to bring about the connection with different levels of the upper world, with the planetary spheres. The sevenfold sacrificial flames on the mountain top and the sevenfold rising of incense are to transport Balaam's soul to the heights of spiritual vision.

'And Balaam said to Balak, "Stand beside your burnt offering, and I will go; perhaps the Lord will come to meet me; and whatever he shows me I will tell you." And he went to a bare height.'

This 'going' of Balaam to a meeting with God is not to be taken merely physically; it is a 'going out' of his soul from his body through the power of the seven burnt offerings. Nor is the fact that meanwhile Balak is to 'stand beside' the burnt offerings without inner significance. While Balaam's soul is on the 'bare height', the king is to carry on the sacrifice from the earth and give it spiritual support.

Balaam's 'going' does in fact lead to a meeting, and the first words he speaks to the deity are: 'I have prepared the seven altars, and I have offered upon each altar a bull and a ram.' This means that the seven altars were the last earthly impression he had taken with him, that it was by the power of this image that he knew he was carried into higher worlds. And God 'put a word in Balaam's mouth' and commanded him to return and pronounce it to Balak.

'And he returned to him, and lo, he and all the princes of Moab were standing beside his burnt offering.' (23:6). The seer's soul returns from its ecstatic state, descends once more into his body. As if out of clouds the earthly surroundings take shape before his eyes. The earthly world gradually becomes clear again in the same picture with which it faded away; with the sight of this solemn ritual the soul feels its way back to earthly existence. There is Balak standing beside the burnt offering and all the princes 'standing beside' it are like the priestly assistants at High Mass; their hierarchical grouping is like a picture of the higher worlds.

Now Balaam speaks what has been revealed to him; the seer becomes the magician who speaks forth words of power. It is not a curse, however, but a blessing he delivers.

Thereupon Balak leads him to another high place, Mount Pisgah. The same thing happens again. Once more Balaam does not bring a curse but a blessing.

4 The pronouncements

Balak led the seer to three mountains, led him in three different ways into 'higher' states of consciousness, for each mountain reaches up into higher worlds in a different way.

45

The word from above, the inspiration, is thus received in different ways.

The pronouncements Balaam makes become more substantial and more forceful each time. This corresponds to the fact that he increasingly becomes an instrument of good powers, and that his own magic practices, his 'sorcery', decrease more and more the clearer the revelation flows. It is part of the subtlety of this account that the experiences on the three mountains also become more impressive as they proceed: three times the same thing seems to happen and yet each time the apparent sameness has a different shading. The first time Balaam has to 'go' to a meeting with God. The second time he simply waits, the third time 'he did not go, as at other times, to meet with omens' but 'the Spirit of God came upon him'. His own deeds become increasingly insignificant the more firmly he becomes an instrument of higher spiritual beings who lead evolution towards Christ and who can transform evil to good, and curse to blessing.

In his first pronouncement he recognizes the special status of the people of Israel in that it cannot be reckoned among the other peoples.

The second points even more clearly to the coming Messiah: 'The LORD their God is with them, and the shout of a king is among them.' (23:21). And after the golden clarion ring of the word 'king' there shines out with sunlike power the picture of the lion raising itself up — an anticipation of the sunlike conqueror and vanquisher of death spoken of by John in the Book of Revelation (5:5): 'lo, the Lion of the tribe of Judah . . . has conquered . . .'

The third pronouncement begins with all solemnity. Balaam sees the twelve tribes encamped in the wilderness. They are like the constellations in heaven. As it is in heaven, so also on the earth. Thereupon his visionary power this time really takes fire. Heavenly mysteries are revealed to him. Before his visionary eye the wilderness becomes the garden of paradise. In this third pronouncement there lies an anticipation of how the Messiah will bring about the 're-enlivening' of the wilderness of 'dying earth existence', and from far off appears the picture of the heavenly 'gardener' who works in the garden of the Resurrection. The Water of Life flows through this third pronouncement. Immediately on sight of the wilderness this prophecy comes to him (24:5–9):

> *How fair are your tents, O Jacob,*
> > *your encampments, O Israel!*

The poor tents become the heavenly 'houses' of the zodiac.

> *Like valleys that stretch afar,*
> > *like gardens beside a river,*
> *like aloes that the LORD has planted,*
> > *like cedar trees beside the waters.*
> *Water shall flow from his buckets,*
> > *and his seed shall be in many waters.*

Finally, after the sign of the lion once more,

> *Blessed be every one who blesses you,*
> > *and cursed be every one who curses you.*

Balak grows angry and refuses the seer the reward of honour since he has not cursed but blessed the enemy. But then Balaam is inspired to a fourth pronouncement, and in this he soars to the very heights. Again there is the solemn prologue, but even more far-reaching than in the third pronouncement (24:15f).

> *And he took up his discourse, and said,*
> *'The oracle of Balaam the son of Beor,*
> > *the oracle of the man whose eye is opened,*
> *the oracle of him who hears the words of God,*
> > *and knows the knowledge of the Most High,*
> *who sees the vision of the Almighty,*
> > *falling down, but having his eyes uncovered.'*

The extent of spiritual vision depends upon the degree of reverence in man. He falls to his knees and so has his 'eyes uncovered'.

And now there comes in this fourth pronouncement the

47

prophecy of the 'star'. The shining star of grace, that the wise men from the east are to see when the time is ripe, Balaam sees already, more than a thousand years beforehand. The future already exists spiritually, though simply as something coming towards the present, more or less distant from it. Balaam feels that he now sees what belongs to a far distant future (24:17).

> *I see him, but not now;*
> *I behold him, but not nigh:*
> *a star shall come forth out of Jacob . . .*

What follows may sound violently warlike. We are still in the Old Testament. The seer is able to perceive above all how the coming of the Messiah will be a judgment, and shall 'break down all the sons of Sheth [chaos]'. He sees how the coming of the Messiah will bring about the defeat of all those who would like to make the earth a godless chaos, free of the divine jurisdiction, and who do not want the star of peace to descend to earth. The seer of ancient times cannot yet, however, discern how the Messiah will appear with no weapon other than the victorious power of inner sacrifice, how the power of the Lion will come in the form of the Lamb. The Revelation of John says: ' . . . lo, the Lion . . . has conquered . . .' 'And I saw a Lamb . . .' The seer of ancient times has only the images of military conquests, but the mighty sunlike power with which they are invested is the same that at a later time will be revealed in the 'Lamb of God'. And above all the star is the same which will sparkle and shed its light over Bethlehem.

> *I see him, but not now;*
> *I behold him, but not nigh:*
> *star shall come forth . . .*

In these words there reaches us from a dim and distant past a very early anticipation of what Christ said to John on Patmos (Rev. 22:16): 'I am . . . the bright morning star.'

6. 'I lift up my eyes to the hills . . .'
(Psalm 121)

1

The words 'I lift up my eyes to the hills' express one of man's primal religious experiences. They form the opening of Psalm 121, which in all its simplicity is a classic religious document.

It belongs to a group of Psalms each headed: 'A Song of Ascents', pilgrim songs that were sung when people went up to the holy hill-city of Jerusalem. Physical and spiritual pilgrimage were inseparable in the experience of men of those days. Outwardly as well as inwardly it meant a going upwards, an 'elevation'. The pious uplifted gaze of the distant pilgrim quite naturally began to 'see' in a higher sense.

'I lift up my eyes . . .' The animals also have eyes; some animals are even superior to man in the penetrating keenness of their vision. The animal, however, cannot so unselfishly give itself up to pure 'looking' as man. This is expressed physiologically in the fact that animals' eyes have a stronger blood supply, are more part of the actual life processes. An animal's seeing is always somehow determined by its biology. Its looking always has something to do with its own interests and is concerned with its main task of survival. The eye of man enables him simply to look with absolute objectivity and thus he can get quite free of himself and the needs of his own organism. He is able to raise his eyes to the distant hills.

In the original text the second line does not follow in the way that is so familiar from Authorized or Prayer Book versions of the Psalms: 'from whence cometh my help.' I is a question: 'Whence does my help come?' This question arises from looking at the distant hills. Looked at aright they point beyond themselves and allow a sense of the divine. It is by no means superfluous to draw attention to the fact that the order of the sentences is not reversed. It is not: 'Whence comes help to me? So I lift my eyes and look for help from God above.' The starting point for true religion is not the necessity that causes man to seek for help, the danger that teaches prayer. The starting point of Psalm 121 is the religious experience of the divine that follows from looking up to the holy hills. This lies a plane higher than merely being in need of help; it is the selfless sphere of altruistic worship. If, then, as a result of this devoted gaze the question arises: 'Whence does my help come?' it is not connected with the individual needs but the basic, primal need that arises from our human nature in the presence of the divine: in looking up I first become aware that I am not as I should be, that my humanity is incomplete. This calls for a decisive help which can come to me only from above. The chief thing is not that this or that wish is fulfilled, but that I myself am fulfilled.

This insight grows in a true and legitimate way with the very striving. Only one who makes a great effort comes through it to the point where he knows the indispensability of grace, the 'love from above'.* The question born out of looking up to the hills: 'Whence does my help come?' is asking for that love from above. 'Whence comes what is *the* help for my innate being?' If as Christians we adopt the psalm, we may complete it by affirming that this decisive help for our human nature has come to us in Christ. The name 'Jesus' even means 'God's help'. In Christ Jesus *the* help descends to us which alone can do enough for the primal need of our needy humanity.

*A phrase from Goethe's *Faust* often used by Rudolf Frieling.

Since the question about help first arose from looking up
to the divine, it quite naturally penetrates into higher regions
where it answers itself. As if it were an inspiration from
those distant hills, the questioner hears what is really like
something he says to himself in his higher ego: 'My help —
from the LORD!' (literal trans.)

The 'LORD' — *Yahweh* in Hebrew, *Kyrios* in the Greek
translation — already indicates the sphere of Christ. But the
looking up to the hills that enlarges the soul makes it at once
clear to the Psalmist that this Lord is not only the ruler of
our soul but at the time is the universal world-ego. He it is
who 'made heaven and earth'. The vision of the help-
bringing God therefore broadens into the one who encompasses the whole universe.

> *A Song of Ascents.*
> *I lift up my eyes to the hills.*
> *From whence does my help come?*
> *My help comes from the LORD,*
> *who made heaven and earth.*

2

The pious inner dialogue leads on to hearing a 'voice' that
presses upon the ear of the soul from the spiritual world
itself — in a higher sense 'from without to within'. The
answer to the question was experienced as arising within
the questioner's own ego so that he spoke to himself: 'My
help comes from the LORD . . .' Now comes the step from
talking to oneself to being spoken to from a higher world
that begins to disclose itself. 'He will not let your foot be
moved'. Just before it says: '*My* eyes . . . *my* help . . .',
now suddenly: '*your* foot . . . keeps *you*'.

Now the Psalmist is no longer so obviously in his own
body as to consider it a personal possession but, as if from
the spiritual world, looks at his earthly being from the
opposite direction.

He will not let your foot be moved,
  he who keeps you will not slumber.
Behold, he who keeps Israel
  will neither slumber nor sleep.

With our feet we walk our life's path. Once we have learnt
to walk we are normally no longer conscious of it. Our feet
go downstairs correctly, they even find their way over dark
uneven ground, they are often in advance of our conscious
attention with the sureness of the sleepwalker. But then
there can be an unexpected stumble or slip that brings
unimagined consequences in its train. All this does not lie
entirely in our conscious control; the unconscious plays a
part in it. In this case the ever-wakeful divine consciousness
must help to complement man's inadequate awareness; it is
awake where we are asleep.

God does not sleep. What does this really mean? What
does 'sleep' mean? The usual attitude today is that a man
asleep is in some way diminished, deprived of the something
that makes him conscious and capable of action. He has
shrunk as it were. In reality his soul has gone out of him to
dwell among higher beings who now strengthen, heal and
renew the sleeping soul given into their care, as well as the
body left without consciousness. We sleep only because
there is something higher into which we enter and immerse
ourselves. We need something 'into' which we can sleep.
God is the highest being. He does not sleep — for into what
should *he* sleep? He is himself the all-embracing. He has his
rest and support within himself; he does not need to immerse
himself in another, but can ever receive all other beings into
himself so that they take rest from their separate beings in
him, so that they find new life, new creation in him. One
can never truly rest but 'in God'. In order that he who sleeps
can rest in God, God must be awake for him. What goes on
partly in the sleeping-unconscious even while we are awake,
like the movement of the feet, is also in the Psalm entrusted
to this being who is awake for everyone. 'He will not let

your foot be moved'. From mysterious depths he will grant a safe journey through life and prevent 'false steps'.

Again the one who prays is led beyond the personal to the general: he who keeps him also keeps Israel. He certainly has his personal relation to each individual, but one should never lose sight of the fact that over and above that he is the guardian of much wider circles. In Christian terms he is the keeper of mankind.

3

In its characteristic way of linking thoughts together our Psalm again takes up the 'keeper' motif in the third stanza:

> The LORD is your keeper:
>   the LORD is your shade
>   on your right hand.
> The sun shall not smite you by day,
>   nor the moon by night.

To those of us who live in northern countries where the sunlight is not so strong, 'shade' suggests something negative, a looming of the realm of darkness into the brightness of day. One must have done harvesting on a hot August day to appreciate what a blessing it can be if only for a moment a cloud takes away the merciless heat. One can then understand how the overshadowing clouds with their refreshing coolness were experienced in the lands of the Bible. In this sense Luke speaks of the overshadowing of Mary by the Holy Spirit. In this sense the Psalm speaks of the overshadowing of our hand by the divine. It is the right hand, with which every day we have to engage in shaping our earthly existence. God watches over the traveller, he shades the worker. Man's creative hand needs this protection so that its activity can be beneficial.

This positive aspect of shade also enables us to understand the next verse which speaks of the warding off of harmful influences. Just as at high noon the intense rays of the sun can harm a man, so too, we are told, can the full moon shining with unclouded brilliance from the zenith at midnight in more southerly lands. For us sunstroke and moonstroke can stand for all harmful influences that threaten destruction by day or by night.

4

The Psalm has spoken of the eyes, the foot, the hand. It is as if it went through the whole threefold organization of man: the thinking head — the earth-treading foot — the hand whose creativeness comes from the middle region, the heart. In a fourth stanza the theme is taken up again and in three final sentences drawn to a grand conclusion.

First, the protection from 'all evil'. As with the seventh request of the Lord's Prayer it would be too superficial to think only of being protected from misfortunes that come to us from without. In the deeper Christian sense it is not only the evil that is done to us, but that above all to which we are prone in our own souls insofar as we are possessed by egoism. The dark possibility of doing evil is also always connected with the wonderful possibility of being aware of our own individuality, of saying 'I'.

From here we proceed to the 'soul',* which with its whole range of feeling is submitted to the divine protection, and lastly to the 'going out and coming in', which again refers us to the earthly journey, this time considered in its rhythm of going and coming, of setting out and returning home. We find this rhythm throughout life, in small things and in greater ones. We find it in the morning departure and the evening homecoming, in breathing out and breathing in, in sleeping and waking, in being born and dying. Coming into the world is seen from above as going out of a higher world, and death as the homecoming. From the earth

---

*Thus also AV and Prayer Book. RSV has 'life' for the Hebrew *nephesh*.

incarnation is seen as coming in, and death as going out, the '*exitus*'.

These life rhythms afford at the end of the Psalm the far view into the timeless, the eternal: 'from this time forth and for evermore.' In order to appreciate the meaning of this ancient religious expression anew perhaps instead of 'time' one should try using the word 'instant' for its more immediate effect. Between the past and the future stands the 'instant' — which can be seized only by real 'presence' of mind. For whoever grasps the instant in spiritual awareness there opens at the same time a window into the timeless: 'from this instant on' and for evermore.

As in the first stanza looking up to the hills leads out into the distances of space, so in the last the grasping of the rhythmical world leads towards the distances of time, and thence into eternity.

> *The LORD will keep you from all evil;*
> *he will keep your life [soul].*
> *The LORD will keep*
> *your going out and your coming in*
> *from this time [instant] forth and for evermore.*

7. Experience of God
(Psalm 63)

'A Psalm of David, when he was in the Wilderness of Judah.' The desert is part of the world that seems to have fallen away from the great organism of life, to be lost to the powers of creation. David experienced the wilderness in nature. People today experience it in great cities, in the domain of the death of a civilization that makes existence lifeless and desolate. 'The desert grows — woe to him who fosters deserts' said Nietzsche.

Over three thousand years later the words of the Psalm that was prayed in the desert of Judea can still speak to us.

The Psalm begins with the cry: 'O God . . .' All around the powers of death are triumphant — the search for God must therefore lead within. There something stirs that is connected with the living God: 'Thou deity of my innermost being . . .' (Author's translation).

'I seek thee' (RSV) or 'early will I seek thee' (AV). The word 'dawn' is contained in the Hebrew verb here. If the human self becomes conscious of its basic connection with the divine self, there is something like a dawning in the soul. Just as the dawn precedes the rising of the sun, there begins to glow in the soul the feeling of a great awakening. In the world of external nature God's sun has already risen aeons ago; the innermost part of man is still virgin land to God. There the sun is to rise more and more in the future. This is why the start of each awakening of the soul is like a sacred dawn.

From this meeting with God in the innermost self the Psalm now turns to man's life of feeling. The religion of the one who prayed this Psalm was of such an elementary nature that he could allow all the feelings and strivings, all the wishes and yearnings of his soul to converge in one mighty longing for the divine: 'my soul thirsts for thee.'

Then he descends to the earthly body of flesh and blood, and is able to include that too as part of his devotion. The body does not, as so often with us, 'make a nuisance of itself' when the soul wants to soar upwards. It is not in the way; even its weakness is part of the basic religious experience. Its feebleness is experienced as the need for God, as instinctive craving for God. The unspoiled human body can experience the satisfying of hunger and the quenching of thirst with devotion; so here the physical privation is experienced as desire for God.

> O God!
> Thou — deity of my innermost being!
> The dawning in my soul awakes to thee.
> My soul thirsts for thee.
> My body faints for need of thee
> In a land without water, dry and parched.
> (Author's translation)

The solitary desert prayer is now supported by remembrance of the experience of the cult in the sanctuary. In the cult what the physical eye sees is so arranged that the visionary power of the soul is left free. This is a further indication in the Psalms of the experience of the supersensory that can arise at the sight of the holy rites.

> So I have looked upon thee in the sanctuary,
> beholding thy power and glory.

The one who prays in the desert feels a surrender of his awakened being to the divine revelation such as he has otherwise felt only when he was present in body and soul at the holy sacrificial rite.

In this experience of the divine glory the 'love from above' comes to him and confers on him a feeling of completely new life. What he otherwise called 'his life' loses importance. When that highest good has shone in his heart, he may say on looking at his ordinary daily life: 'Life is not the highest good.' So the Psalm says: 'Thy steadfast love is better than life.'

It is to this love that 'praise' is now given. In order to feel once more the original freshness of this overworn religious word, we may consider the following. People today are predominantly critically minded. They strengthen their self-esteem by criticizing, but the soul cannot be thus satisfied. In order to be healthy it needs to look up to that world which is 'better than life'. It needs to be able to be enthusiastic about something. In this way it achieves the opposite of criticism: the recognition that grows into worship. Perhaps, then, we today can understand religious praise as the positive counterpart of the critical attitude that destroys and impoverishes the individual soul. The praise of the lips goes on to become 'blessing' — 'So I will bless thee as long as I live.'

There arises quite naturally and automatically at this point the religious gesture of raising the hands. We know it from the Act of Consecration of Man. If you raise your hands to heaven, you reach out beyond yourself. That can only properly be done 'in the name' of God as the Psalm expresses it (AV). This name stands for all that can be present of God in the one who recognizes him. It grows into a true communion, an inner receiving of the divine being, which he who prays 'eats and drinks', which thus permeates his flesh and blood.

> *Because thy loving kindness is better than life,*
> *my lips shall praise thee.*
> *Thus will I bless thee while I live:*
> *I will lift up my hands in thy name.*
> *My soul shall be satisfied as with marrow and fatness;*
> *and my mouth shall praise thee with joyful lips. (AV)*

This experience of dawn then works into the hours of night. In the 'night watches' it proves its power. He who watches with religious devotion during the time of sleep —

we may think of the midnight service at Christmas — seeks at least to reach consciously those heights that his soul otherwise enters unconsciously when it is freed from the body during sleep. What is it that the waking soul does at night according to the Psalm? The Hebrew word is *hagah*, rendered in both the Authorised and Revised Standard Versions as 'meditate'. He who piously fills the watches of the night in this way experiences the security of being under the 'wings' of God.

God spreads his wings protectingly over the soul. But man is not only the passive object of this protective care. Something in him reaches towards God — 'My soul clings to thee'. The Hebrew word for 'clings' has become an important concept in Jewish mysticism — *'devequth'*. The Spanish cabbalist, Isaac of Acre (*c.* 1300), tells the story of a student who seeks the mysteries of the inner life and is asked by his master whether he has yet achieved perfect equanimity of soul. He answers: 'Indeed, I feel satisfaction at praise and pain at insult, but I am not revengeful and bear no grudge.' That, however, does not satisfy the master. 'My son, go back to your home, for as long as you have no equanimity and can still feel the sting of insult, you have not attained to the state where you can connect your thoughts with God.'* This story may shame many a Christian. Only above that stratum of the soul where the pain of insult is felt lies the possibility of 'clinging to God'.

God spreads out his wings. The soul 'clings to God' — so that God can respond with a fresh deed of grace: 'Thy right hand upholds me.' This picture of the divine right hand holding us has something still more personal than the spreading of wings — not only protection but also support, which flows into us through this hand, giving us also power to support ourselves.

*G.G. Scholem, *Major Trends in Jewish Mysticism*, p. 97.

> *. . . I think of thee upon my bed,*
> *and meditate on thee in the watches of the night;*
> *For thou hast been my help,*
> *and in the shadow of thy wings I sing for joy.*
> *My soul clings to thee;*
> *thy right hand upholds me.*

But now there comes a discordant note in the pure harmony of this wonderful prayer, a typical 'Old Testament' note, in the reference to the persecutors who head for their own perdition. 'But those that seek my soul, to destroy it . . . shall fall by the sword' (AV). One must certainly think of what actually gave rise to this: David's flight into the Judean Desert, though the pursuers of those times can have only a purely historical interest for us today. But as the 'Desert of Judea' becomes for us the modern 'desert experience', so from a religious point of view David's pursuers represent today's opposing forces, the powers of the Adversary. There is a deep inner truth in the fact that they have their place in such a song of divine love. It is an age old experience that the closer one comes to God the stronger becomes the sensitivity to what opposes him. It is therefore just at its climax in Communion that the Act of Consecration of Man is mindful of the 'Adversary'.

It is not merely fortuitous that this passage is preceded by the verse about being upheld by God's right hand. He who feels thus upheld can now view the evil powers undismayed. In the Apocalypse of John the Christian seer looks upon the adversaries, and learns that the beast from the abyss will 'go to perdition' (17:8). Spiritual observation of this creature's inner motivation reveals where it is heading. The seer sees that it can come to no good end.

So the Psalmist sees that the servants of the enemy are on the road to perdition. They are intent upon the 'destruction' of his soul — so says the Psalm literally. 'The destruction of the soul' — this expression once coined by David in relation to actual hostile people is for us no longer connected with a long past feud, but acts as an appropriate pointer to certain powers. There are in fact erring spiritual powers that aim at the devastation of the human soul. Above all they are at work where 'the desert grows' — within and without. All soul destruction happens in a world that can truly be called an 'underworld'. Wherever the powers of the soul and warmth of heart die out, we are in reality no longer living in a world lit by the sun, but in a 'sub-earthly' realm.

Two further images are added — the sword and the jackal. Those who are on the way to 'the depths of the earth', to Hades, fall victim to the 'sword'. In an apocalyptic sense this is the sword of the spirit as it went forth from the mouth of the 'white rider' and overcame the Adversary. 'Prey for jackals' — this too can become an apocalyptic picture, whatever may once have been meant literally. Such noxious, carrion-eating creatures can become an image of demonic beings that feed not on the decomposing body but on all the inner elements of decay that proceed from the departing soul, beings that feed themselves as it were by means of the badness that a soul brings with it. The reference to the night-howling jackal allows a glimpse into this sinister world.

> But those who are intent to destroy my soul
>   are on the way to the lower parts of the earth,
> to fall by the sword,
>   prey for jackals. (Author's translation)

The light is all the brighter again against this gloomy background. Now comes a word that has not been heard before in the psalm: 'the king'. Again we may look beyond the person of David and regard 'king' as an expression for an exalted state of humanity — rather as the Apocalypse speaks of Christ making us 'priests and kings'. 'But the king shall rejoice in God.' For us this sounds like the Gospel of John speaking of the joy of Christ. All the religious strength of feeling hitherto expressed in the Psalm — the longing for God, the seeing of God, the devotion, the sense of being fed, protected, supported — finally condenses into the 'rejoicing in God', which cannot even be extinguished in the face of the enemy.

Not so immediately accessible to the modern reader perhaps is the conclusion of the whole Psalm: accounting blessed those who 'swear by' the king, and the reference to the stopping of 'the mouths of liars'. If the Psalm is read from a Christian point of view, the 'king' is Christ himself. He bears in him the Logos, the world-creating Word. The motif of 'swearing' indicates a mystery of the word. The man who swears summons the presence of higher beings, his word 'under oath' is spoken in their immediate presence. Just as the Greek and Latin word for 'conscience' means a 'knowing-with' (*syn-eidon, con-scientia*) higher beings, so swearing means a 'speaking-with' the invisible. He therefore who swears by the 'king' summons the king to speak with him, he takes up into his human word something of the creative divine Word itself.

In connection with these mysteries of the divine power of the Word we can also come to a proper understanding of the last sentence of the Psalm, which says that 'the mouths of liars will be stopped'. After the experience of the holy, creative word of God the satanic character of the lie is all the more apparent. The Zarathustran religion of ancient Persia had a very strong sense that it was Ahriman, the enemy of the gods, who was active in the lie. The activity of deceitful powers is a terrible evil. The prophecy that these forces opposed to the divine Word are one day to be deprived of their power by him voices a great apocalyptic hope, and as such is a worthy conclusion to this song in celebration of man's experience of God.

> *But the king shall rejoice in God;*
> *all who swear by him shall glory;*
> *for the mouths of liars will be stopped.*

8. 'I shall not die, but I shall live'
(Psalm 118 — an Easter hymn)

1

It is a moving moment when Matthew's Gospel (23:39) describes how Christ bade farewell to his public ministry in order to devote the last day before his Passion solely to his disciples. In this farewell to the multitude on Maundy Thursday he says: 'For I tell you, you will not see me again, until you say, "Blessed is he who comes in the name of the Lord." '

His activity in an earthly body visible to all men draws to an end. 'You will not see me again with earthly eyes.' As the Risen One, however, he is to 'come' to men in a new way and be present to them. In order to be able to perceive him in this supersensory form people will need a new supersensory organ of vision. 'You will not see me again, until you say, "Blessed is he who comes . . . ".' 'Until you say . . .' which means: when you speak this prayer of greeting not only with your lips but from your whole being, then its words will enable you to see my coming in supersensory form. This holy prayer of greeting that makes the human soul ready to receive and perceive the coming Christ stems from the Old Testament, from the Psalm which those of Christ's time clearly felt to indicate the future Saviour.

It was on Palm Sunday as he entered Jerusalem that the multitude first received the Saviour with this prayer of greeing from Psalm 118. Out of the dimly felt greatness of the historic moment the crowd, lifted beyond itself as if drawn up into a corporate clairvoyance, had given voice to these words: 'Blessed be he who comes in the name of the Lord! Hosanna in the highest!' The instinctive clairvoyance that burst upon the soul in that special moment on Palm Sunday could nevertheless not be kept alive through Holy Week — on Good Friday the 'Hosanna' even turned into 'Crucify him!' So in his farewell Christ gave men these words for the distant future.

It is good therefore to look for once at the full text of the Psalm that contains such an important saying. As we begin to read it, we are immediately caught by its joyful and elated rhythm. Old Testament scholarship sees it as a kind of festival liturgy divided between different voices and choruses. The Lord has saved the people and the victory is now celebrated with joy and thankfulness. The Psalm therefore begins:

> O give thanks to the LORD, for he is good;
> his steadfast love endures for ever!
>
> Let Israel say,
> 'His steadfast love endures for ever.'
> Let the house of Aaron say,
> 'His steadfast love endures for ever.'
> Let those who fear the LORD say,
> 'His steadfast love endures for ever.'

' . . . for he is good'. The perhaps better-known Prayer Book version here says, ' . . . for he is gracious'. In the original, however, we find in all its nobility the simple but inexhaustible word 'good', with something here of what could be called finality in relation to God himself. It is the word 'good' that rushes from the lips of the rich young man in the Gospel (Mark 10:17f, Luke 18:18f) when he addresses Jesus: 'Good Teacher . . .' He is then faced with the searching question: 'Why do you call me good?' Has the young man discovered the full value of this word? 'No one is good but God alone.' Yet he takes Jesus for a rabbi. He would only have been able to use the word that belongs to God alone if he had seen into the divine depths of Christ's nature. It is in this primal, sublime sense, belonging only to the divine, that this word 'good' is used at the beginning of the Psalm.

The jubilant confession of God's goodness seeks corroboration and confirmation through the community. It appears in three different choruses. First of all 'Israel' is called upon. Then 'the house of Aaron,' the priesthood. Finally all 'who fear the LORD', the great invisible Church of all the religious.

2

In what follows the Psalm singer looks back again to the plight from which God has rescued him. 'Out of my distress I called on the LORD.' Here the translations lack a word that conveys the 'narrowness' which would bring out the force of the imagery of verse five. Though archaic, the word 'strait' rather than 'distress' would still perhaps convey the meaning of the Hebrew most directly. We get the picture of a gorge in which the ever closer-leaning rock walls give the feeling of suffocation. It was from this distressing sense of constriction that the cry for help to God arose. The soul once descended from the bright expanses of the heavenly worlds. Now it finds itself in the narrow, rocky gorge of earthly existence, confined by egoism, restricted by life in a hardened material body. It anxiously gasps as it were for air to breathe.

Now the imagery contrasts 'narrowness' with 'width'. The impact is lost without the contrast, and where the meaning is most closely rendered in the Prayer Book version its expression is somewhat ambiguous for the modern ear: 'and the Lord heard me *at large*' (that is, without restraint or confinement). Man is confined and restricted; God responds from a state just the opposite. Divine comfort comes to the troubled soul from the 'widths'. It is one of the very first elements of religion: the soul in earthly confinement calling on the divine — the divine answering from the light-filled heavenly expanses. (The AV and RSV translations gloss this over with their 'and set me in a large place' and 'set me free').

Following this response from the divine widths there comes the jubilant cry: 'The LORD is on my side'. In the original there is simply God's name and abruptly next to it the dative 'to me': 'The LORD — to me!' It is almost as if this were the original formulation of the dative case, so vital is its use. It will be repeated: 'The LORD — to me!'

Whoever experiences this inclining of the divine towards him has nothing to fear. His enemies cannot harm him: 'I shall look in triumph on those who hate me' (RSV), or 'I shall see my desire upon . . .' (AV and Prayer Book). This sounds really 'Old Testamentish'. Strangely, however, the original says only: 'I will look upon my enemies.' We should not necessarily understand the looking to be one of hatred and satisfied vengeance. We may fill this Old Testament expression with the Christian meaning that the gaze of the eyes of absolutely Christian men will one day in the future disarm the Adversary.

Thence arises the triumphant trust in the divine as against all deceptive and illusory repositories of our trust, such as weak men and 'princes'.

> From the strait of my anxiety I called to the LORD.
>> In the widths the LORD gave answer.
> The LORD — to me! He inclined towards me.
>> Nothing do I fear.
>> What can men do to me?
> The LORD — to me! He inclined towards me.
>> Mine is his help,
>> Mine to look on those that hate me.

> *It is good to trust the LORD,*
> *better than trusting in men.*
> *It is good to trust the LORD,*
> *better than trusting in princes.*
>
> (118:5–9. *Author's translation*)

3

Once again there is an echo of the affliction undergone. The afflicters, the 'heathen', translated from Old Testament into universally human terms, are the powers of the Adversary. The cry of triumph rings out three times: 'In the name of the LORD I cut them off!' It is the experience that reaches its Christian climax in the words of the sacrament at Communion: the power of the Adversary is taken from us when we shelter within the name of Christ. The name is then certainly not just a word but is that in which the presence of the divine being is recognized with full consciousness. The powers that want to bring about man's fall by constantly renewed temptation are put to flight by this sheltering within the holy Name.

> *All nations surrounded me;*
> *in the name of the LORD I cut them off!*
> *They surrounded me, surrounded me on every side;*
> *in the name of the LORD I cut them off!*
> *They surrounded me like bees,*
> *they blazed like a fire of thorns;*
> *in the name of the LORD I cut them off!*
> *I was pushed hard, so that I was falling,*
> *but the LORD helped me.*
> *The LORD is my strength and my song;*
> *he has become my salvation.* (118:10–14)

4

Now the rejoicing breaks out again. 'Hark, glad songs . . .' Only song is able to capture the soul's tremendous feeling of joy. 'The right hand of the LORD does valiantly.' The right hand is the embodiment of 'action'. The Old Testament motif of divine acts of salvation first finds its completion in God's unique, death-conquering deed on Golgotha. Psalm 118 first gains its full meaning as an Easter hymn.

This relation to the Easter joy of Christianity comes to light very clearly once more. In verse seventeen we enter the Holy of Holies: 'I shall not die, but I shall live'. The Psalm touches on the great mystery of life and death and expresses the certainty that man finally belongs on the side of life, that he is destined for eternity.

In this eternal life he will not exist only for his own sake but will serve the further revelation of the being of God. 'And recount the deeds of the LORD' need not be anything to do with the spoken word. It proclaims God's deed, and the proof of it in mankind's own resurrection.

The Psalmist knows full well that he has not yet reached the goal. He still needs the trials and tribulations. 'The LORD has chastened me sorely . . .' But these painful blows of destiny will only awaken and chasten and so serve the higher life.

> Hark, glad songs of victory
> > in the tents of the righteous;
> 'The right hand of the LORD does valiantly,
> > the right hand of the LORD is exalted,
> > the right hand of the LORD does valiantly!'
> I shall not die, but I shall live,
> > and recount the deeds of the LORD.
> The LORD has chastened me sorely,
> > but he has not given me over to death.
> > > (118: 15–18, author's emphasis)

5

After the breaking through of Easter certainty — as could hardly be otherwise in the wonderfully organic series of pictures — doors that were previously closed begin to open.

If one looks at the Psalm in relation to its historical background, one can naturally suppose that at this point in the great festival liturgy of victory the procession of celebrants has arrived in front of the Temple and demands entry. 'Open to me the gates of righteousness.' But this does not exhaust the meaning of the sentence. The expression 'gates of righteousness' indicates that the Temple doors become images of more exalted doorways. Higher worlds are about to open up.

'Righteousness' is not complacent correctness. We speak of work or material being right or correct. 'Right' is what fits like a trimmed stone in building so that one can make use of it. 'Right' is what exists in accord with the divine harmony of the universe. Therefore only the righteous can pass through the doors. 'The gates of righteousness' then become 'the gate of the LORD'. All the harmony of the universe ultimately has its origin in Christ himself.

Nor should we overlook how soon 'humility'* is mentioned after 'righteousness'. The righteous for whom these gates are to be opened are yet not fit for the divine world if they are not capable of humility.

> Open to me the gates of righteousness!
> I will go through them
> to praise the LORD.
> This is the gate of the LORD.
> The righteous go through it.
> I praise thee who hast made me humble
> and art my salvation.   (118:19–21. Author's translation)

*This word does not appear in the English translations, AV, RSV and Prayer Book.

6

After this mention of humility there appears the puzzling image of 'The stone which the builders rejected' which 'has become the chief cornerstone.' God himself in his Messiah offers the greatest example of humility. Here we find the presentiment that the Messiah when he comes does not seize power unopposed and as a matter of course, but remains inconspicuous. So much so that he lays himself open to misunderstanding and rejection. Out of love for our freedom. On Maundy Thursday, Christ Jesus himself quotes these words from the Psalm in direct connection with the sombre parable of the evil workers in the vineyard who kill the beloved son of the owner. Christ knew that it was just as the Rejected and Condemned that he would build the new temple in the Resurrection — first of all the temple of his resurrection body, which is moreover the beginning of the great and all-embracing resurrection denoted by the 'heavenly Jerusalem'. This word 'cornerstone' therefore contains a Christian mystery of 'building' that first becomes recognizable in the light of the Easter events. 'The LORD brought this about; it is a marvel to our eyes' — words with which even today Christendom can express its awed astonishment in face of the Easter event; then Easter is *the* marvel.

Through the marvel the eternal enters the temporal. Thereby time becomes something different; it takes on a content of eternity that almost breaks through it. A new 'day' shines as once the first day of creation shone in the primal divine light. Easter Day is this new day, which emerges as if directly from God's hands and which seeks its glorification in the radiant joy of the redeemed soul.

> *A stone — the builders rejected it.*
> *It has become the cornerstone!*
> *The LORD brought this about,*
> *a marvel to our eyes.*

This is the day — the LORD has made it.
  Let us rejoice!
  Let us be glad of it! (118:22–24. Author's translation)

7

The multitude felt that a true Sunday glory shone around them on Palm Sunday, the octave of which is Easter Day. Walking in the light of the day which 'the LORD has made' the people give voice to the verse of greeting: 'Blessed be he who comes in the name of the Lord!' The 'Hosanna' that is linked to it is, like 'Amen' and 'Halleluia', one of the Hebrew words that the New Testament did not translate into Greek but retained with the full force of their original sound. 'Hosanna' means 'Save us!' — 'Blessed be . . .' in its Latin form, together with 'hosanna', has entered into the Mass and the great musical settings of the Mass: '*Benedictus qui venit in nomine Domini*'. Bruckner's Mass in F minor for example shows most beautifully what a wealth of devotional Christian feeling has sprung from these words.

In the Psalm there now follows an expression that in connection with the Old Testament festival procession was apparently spoken to those entering by the priests waiting in the Temple. 'We bless you from the house of the LORD.' One could thus conclude that the preceding sentence, 'Blessed be he . . .', did not necessarily mean the Messiah, but was intended for the pilgrim who was solemnly approaching the Temple. That sense may also have lain in the words at the time. Clearly, however, it was certainly also felt that this sacred expression bore overtones of yet greater things. The pilgrims who solemnly made their way to the Temple in Jerusalem were ultimately only the forerunners of the One who would one day truly enter his temple — the human body, of which the Temple in Jerusalem was an image. The pious souls of the Old Covenant were able to divine behind the festive band of approaching pilgrims the figure of the great One who should come, the Messiah, the Christ. When later on Judaism was opposed to Christianity, it quite intentionally allowed such 'Messianic' references in the Old Testament to fall into the background. But it is evident from the behaviour of the crowd on Palm Sunday that this verse, 'Blessed be he who comes . . .', was once applied to the Messiah.

What, then, from our standpoint is meant by the twenty-seventh verse: 'The LORD is God, and he has given us light'? Such a verse is an attestation of visionary experiences in the religious worship of the ancient past. Through true religious worship men were once able to behold the presence of the god. At the climax came the 'Epiphany', the appearance of the god before the celebrants. Then gradually in the course of time these faculties of vision died out. They came to life again in a certain way in the Christian era, since up until the Middle Ages some Christians had a direct experience through the sacrament of the actual coming of Christ. Such experiences will again become possible in the future as a result of new forces in man's consciousness. Then an Old Testament expression will again find its full meaning. 'He has given us light'. 'We have beheld his glory' as it is expressed in the prologue of John's Gospel.

In connection with this the Psalm speaks of the green branches that were carried by the participants in the sacred festival procession. This also reminds us of Palm Sunday. Through the green branches nature itself proclaims the great mystery: how from death new life arises. 'I shall live . . .'

> Save us, we beseech thee, O LORD!
>   O LORD, we beseech thee, give us success!
>
> Blessed be he who enters in the name of the LORD!
>   We bless you from the house of the LORD.
> The LORD is God,
>   and he has given us light.

8. 'I SHALL NOT DIE, BUT I SHALL LIVE'

Bind the festal procession with branches,
  up to the horns of the altar!

Thou art my God, and I will give thanks to thee;
thou art my God, I will extol thee.

O give thanks to the LORD, for he is good;
for his steadfast love endures for ever!   (118:25–29)

9. 'Authority to tread upon serpents and scorpions . . .'
(Psalm 91)

'If you are the Son of God, throw yourself down from here; for it is written,

"He will give his angels charge of you, to guard you,"

and

"On their hands they will bear you up,
lest you strike your foot against a stone." '

With these words (Luke 4:9–11) the devil shows that he too can come up with a quotation from Holy Scripture should the need arise. The verse he misuses comes from Psalm 91, and the fact that the tempter can clothe his suggestion in these particular words shows us that they must have been alive in the soul of Jesus of Nazareth. The same Psalm appears once more later in the Gospel when we hear a significant echo of it in Christ's own words: 'I saw Satan fall like lightning from heaven. Behold, I have given you authority to tread upon serpents and scorpions, and over all the power of the enemy; and nothing shall hurt you' (Luke 10:18f).

Psalm 91 therefore plays a unique part in the conflict of Christ with the opposing powers.

The beginning is not easy to translate accurately. The RSV gives: 'He who dwells in the shelter of the Most High . . . will say to the Lord, "My refuge and my fortress . . . " ' In the Hebrew, however, it is not 'He who dwells . . . will say', but 'He who dwells . . . *I* say . . .' The 'I' is preserved in the AV and Prayer Book versions, though both have therefore found it necessary to alter the preceding clause, which in the original is never completed; it hangs in the air without a following main clause. 'He who dwells in the shelter of the Most High and abides in the shadow of the Almighty . . .' — now one has to sense a pause. It is as if in this unfinished introductory sentence a great and wonderful experience were dashed down in advance. It is so overwhelming, the heart is so full of it, that it cannot submit to being confined in a finished grammatical sentence. If we get the impression that something remains hanging in mid-air, that is quite right. In this way it stands like a title over what follows. One could try to include this incomplete, suspended sentence by means of the infinitive:

O — to dwell enveloped in the mystery of the Most High,
to shelter in the shadow of the Almighty . . .

From this experience is born a confession of faith. From it the human ego swings immediately to addressing the divine ego:

I speak to the LORD:
My refuge and my stronghold!
My God in whom I trust.

The fullness and reality of the inner experience expresses itself in the variations of the divine name used. 'The Most High' (*Elyōn*) — the God to whom Melchizedek, the mysterious priest-king of ancient Jerusalem, brought bread and wine was thus named. The 'Almighty' (*Shadai*), likewise called upon already in Abraham's time, was felt to be an especially potent name for the divine life force that can subjugate even the forces of death. 'Lord' denotes the power of the ego within the name 'Yahweh' — in Greek, *Kyrios*. And 'God' is the rendering of *Elohim*, which like a rainbow comprises the many hues of the manifold powers of the divine.

The confession of the psalmist's faith dies away into the divine silence, but out of this silence there arises a sound like an answer. A voice becomes discernible now in return addressing him who sent his words to the supersensory

75

world. It is not yet the voice of God himself, which is to speak at the end of the Psalm, but another voice from the invisible world. It is like the voice of a guardian, an angel sent before the voice of God. It says:

> ' . . . *he will deliver you from the snare of the fowler*
> *and from the deadly pestilence;*
> *he will cover you with his pinions,*
> *and under his wings you will find refuge;*
> *his faithfulness is a shield and a buckler.*
> *You will not fear the terror of the night,*
> *nor the arrow that flies by day,*
> *nor the pestilence that stalks in the darkness,*
> *nor the destruction that wastes at noonday.*
>
> *A thousand may fall at your side,*
> *ten thousand at your right hand;*
> *but it will not come near you.*
> *You will only look with your eyes*
> *and see the recompense of the wicked.*   *(91:3–8)*

On the strength of this voice the Psalmist speaks in his innermost being directly to the Godhead himself:★

Indeed, thou, LORD art my refuge . . .   *(91:9a)*

In comparison with the first confession (verse 2) it shows an enhancement; although there too the 'LORD' is directly addressed, the word 'thou' is nevertheless avoided. This 'thou' — in Hebrew, 'atā', beginning and ending with the vowel 'a' — is like a primal utterance of wonder that there *is* the other ego. The fact that ego-consciousness is not the sole centre of consciousness in the world does not as in Sartrian existentialism appear the prime scandal, but is the source of pious amazement at a divine miracle.

★As in Prayer Book version. In AV and RSV this whole verse appears as part of the words addressed to the Psalmist.

This second confession, which goes so far as to utter the great 'thou', again actuates an inspired hearing of the mysterious 'voice'. It takes up the Psalmist's statement and confirms it. It says:

> . . . *you have made . . .*
> *the Most High your habitation,*
> *no evil shall befall you,*
> *no scourge come near your tent.*
> *For he will give his angels charge of you*
> *to guard you in all your ways.*
> *On their hands they will bear you up,*
> *lest you dash your foot against a stone.*
> *You will tread on the lion and the adder,*
> *the young lion and the serpent you will trample under*
> *foot.* (91:9b–13)

Here too comes an enhancement. The first time the voice conveyed simply a feeling of protection, of refuge, but the pious man is not only to rest in the divine shelter; he is also to be sure of protection in the course of all his activities.

Of course he has to pursue his way on earth, so he cannot be spared also encountering the adverse powers. They make themselves felt for example as 'forces of hindrance' — in our Psalm the 'stone' on the path against which the foot may be dashed. But as instruments of divine Providence angels come to the help of him who is in harmony with the divine. The mysterious 'voice' knows that this help can become so real and effective that the feeling arises of being carried as if by hands over all obstacles.

This is the Scripture the Devil has on his lips when he tempts Christ in the wilderness. As he suggests to him, he should cast himself down from the pinnacle of the Temple, trusting in God. But Christ recognizes the falsification of the lofty words of the Psalm into overweening arrogance, and rejects 'temptation of God'.

On the same spot Christ quotes more from this Psalm at a later stage in his ministry at the moment when the seventy

who had been sent out return from their successful mission
There he speaks of the power to tread on snakes and
scorpions, in a slight variation of the text.

The powers of the Adversary do not only throw stones
in our path through life. They make direct attacks in order
to destroy us — as ravening lions, as venomous snakes. The
lion can also be the image of the most noble and divine
qualities of the heart. Anyone who perceives the heavenly
archetype in the earthly lion will be led to the sublime
Christ-mysteries — to 'the lion who has vanquished'. The
lion of earth, however, does not only reflect the distant
heavenly archetype, but as a physical creature has acquired
destructive powers and lives its life as a fierce beast of prey.
This is how it is seen in the Psalm. And it is from the realm
of feeling centred in the human heart stricken with the
sickness of sin that the 'bad lion' can spring with destructive
violence.

Another quite different aspect of powers hostile to man
is revealed in the poisonous snake that lurks unnoticed on
the path and strikes with its deadly bite. Besides lion and
snake the Psalm looks at another creature that no longer
really exists in the natural world but has its reality in the
invisible. It appears to the soul in dreams as the dragon
(RSV, 'serpent').

The peculiar strength and encouragement of the Psalm —
one could say, its Michaelic character — lies in its being able
to give confidence for life's journey despite all dangers. The
dangers are clearly envisaged. One must know that they
exist — lions, adders, dragons. But if there are demons and
the Devil, then there are also angels. They lift man over the
stone. They enable him to trample evil underfoot and carry
on.

As the inspiring voice reaches these heights of revelation,
it grows silent and gives place to one yet more exalted. To
the two kinds of speech found so far a third is now added.
Speaking himself, the Psalmist said: 'I [the Psalmist] and

thou [God]'. The inspiring voice of the angel said: 'You [the Psalmist] and he [God]'. Now we hear a third voice in which the 'I' of the Godhead himself makes itself heard, whilst the Psalmist is thought of in the third person: 'I [God] and he [the Psalmist]'. God's own voice says:

> *Because he cleaves to me in love, I will deliver him;*
> *I will protect him, because he knows my name.*
> *When he calls to me, I will answer him;*
> *I will be with him in trouble,*
> *I will rescue him and honour him.*
> *With long life I will satisfy him,*
> *and show him my salvation.* (91:14–16)

Here, where the Godhead himself speaks, the Hebrew text resounds with the solemn and majestic word *Anokhi* for 'I'. The 'love from above' can come to the rescue of man because he 'knows' the divine 'name'. God is not 'anonymous' like the world of the atom; with him man is able to know 'whom he is dealing with'. The 'name of God' is the manifestation to us of his innermost nature as it came to us, supremely, in Christ Jesus. If man has become aware of the divine name, then he can be 'extricated' by God above from the toils of a world forfeit to death. He becomes 'transfigured', changed 'from one glory to another' into ever greater glories.

The satisfying with 'long life' at the end of the divine promise we must first translate into the Christian from the Old Testament way of thinking and speaking — to which even divine revelations had to be accommodated. The Old Covenant had the task of preparing the earthly body into which the Saviour could descend and become man. It was therefore in the order of things that the adherants of the Old Covenant should put a high value on their physical existence. The soul would not descend into earthly existence if it did not have a deep-rooted longing for life on earth, a kind of 'hunger'. The life on earth, then, had to fulfil this longing like a satisfying meal. In regard to the patriarchs people certainly had the impression that their deaths came at the moment when they had reached this satisfaction. They died 'old and full of days'. Apart from Abraham and Isaac, this was said only of Job, David and the priest Jehoiada.

In Christianity this special value of earthly existence was not denied but acknowledged still more profoundly. For the religious ancient Hebrews it expressed itself more quantitatively in the 'length' of the allotted life-span, while for us the qualitative aspect is most important — that during our earthly existence we may find Christ and allow ourselves to be permeated by him. The act of redemption itself did not take place in heaven but on earth, and so it is also earthly life that offers the opportunity for becoming Christ-like. Although the human soul stems from heaven and is destined for future heavenly existence, it is here on earth that it has the decisive experience that works on into eternity. This experience satisfies the 'hunger' that leads the soul into earthly existence in order to seek the meaning of life, the 'fullness' of days.

The last sentence of God's words in Psalm 91 opens up the wider horizons of the future. The age of the Holy Spirit, the great awakening of consciousness, is announced. The 'knowing of the divine name' develops into an apocalyptic cosmic vision. 'I will . . . show him my salvation.'

10. The song of the three men in the fiery furnace

The picture of the three men in the fiery furnace is one of the most impressive in the Bible. At the time of the captivity in Babylon in the sixth century BC King Nebuchadnezzar has thrown the three into the furnace for refusing to worship an idol, but the fire does them no harm. Miraculously protected, they walk about freely in the blazing fire and praise God.

Is this a crass product of a 'pious imagination' with a craving for miracles? If so, would our souls be so deeply moved by it? We feel that such a story, which charms us like a fairy tale, is somehow fundamentally true. Like all real fairy tales it has an archetypal quality.*

We find the story in the Old Testament in the third chapter of the Book of Daniel. Not everything is there, however. Among the so-called apocryphal writings there are two additional fragments to the story: 'The Prayer of Azariah' and 'The Song of the Three Young Men'. These texts are not part of the recognized canonical writings of orthodox Judaism or of the Protestant Churches. They belong to a later period than the Book of Daniel and exist only in Greek, stemming from the cosmopolitan Judaism of Alexandria. The Greek translation of the Old Testament, the Septuagint, which also came into existence in Ptolomaic† Alexandria, as well as the much later Latin

*For further study on the background see Bock, *Kings and Prophets*.

†The Ptolemies were originally a Macedonian dynasty that ruled in Egypt as successors of Alexander the Great. They gave a great deal of support to cultural life.

translation of Jerome, the Vulgate, included both these additions as an integral part of the narrative in the third chapter of Daniel. The old Church was guided by a true feeling in acknowledging the addition, for on closer examination it proves to be intimately connected.★

First comes the prayer of Azariah, who is one of the three. He makes himself their spokesman, praying also in their name. Despite the praise it is chiefly a penetential prayer. One must imagine the terrible catastrophe that lay behind the Jews of the Babylonian exile. The flames of burning Jerusalem, the flames of the burning Temple had lighted their way into the misery of exile. All the more unusual that Azariah does not call for vengeance in his prayer, but accepts the catastrophe in humility of heart as inflicted by God, indeed not only accepts it, but consents to it. 'Thou hast executed true judgments in all that thou hast brought upon us and upon Jerusalem, the holy city of our fathers.' The Babylonians were only tools of God's judgment. For it is 'because of our sins.' Azariah recognized in the flames of the fire the God who is a 'consuming fire', as the fifth book of Moses says. But by humbly accepting this fate from the hand of God Azariah becomes acquainted with the element of fire. The fire of punishment becomes the flame of purification. Finally within the purifying flame, which burns up everything ungodly, he divines the ardour of God's love. So the flame of sacrifice is kindled in Azariah's soul. Since the sanctuary lies in ashes, the Temple rites are necessarily in abeyance, but for that reason the sacrifice has

★In the Roman Catholic ritual the Song of the Three Young Men plays an important part in that it appears four times in the year on the so called Quatember Saturdays, on which ordinations of priests also take place. The priest prays the song of praise of the three men, the 'Canticum Benedicite', in the thanksgiving after each Mass. In the old Gallic rite, as it was celebrated up to the eighth century, the hymn was inserted during the reading of each Mass instead of the 'Alleluja'.

The 'Benedicite' is also to be found in the English Book of Common Prayer as an alternative to the 'Te Deum' during Morning Prayer.

to live within men's souls. ' . . . with a contrite heart and a
humble spirit may we be accepted, as though it were with
burnt offerings . . . Such may our sacrifice be in thy sight
this day, and may we wholly follow thee . . .' — words
that have since found their way into the Offertory of the
Sacrament.

Is it for this reason that the flames of the furnace cannot
harm the three, since they have kindled in their hearts the
true fire, the fire of sacrifice born of the purifying, burning
pain of self-knowledge?

As in the Christian sacrament the sacrificial offering of
man is followed by the divinely effected Transubstantiation,
there comes in the experience of the three men after Azariah's
prayer of penitence and offering something yet more
sublime. Outwardly, certainly, it seems as if things were
about to get worse. Provoked by the curiously uninjured
state of the three, those tending the furnace stoke the fire
afresh 'with naphtha, pitch, tow, and brush' so that it burns
as it were seven times hotter than it was before, and the flames
leap seven times seven cubits high. But simultaneously with
the increase of heat the mysterious 'fourth' joins the three,
the 'angel of the Lord' whom Nebuchadnezzar, who also
sees it, calls 'a son of the gods'. He keeps them from
destruction and lets them feel the raging, scorching fire as
'a moist whistling wind'. One is reminded of the Grimm
fairy tale of 'The Old Man Made Young Again' who
'glowed like a rose tree' in the fire and found the blaze like
a 'refreshing dew'.

And now the hymn, 'The Song of the Three Young
Men', follows immediately.★ Azariah is no longer the only
speaker. It is as if the appearance of the mysterious fourth
had conferred on the three the ability of harmoniously
uniting their different soul qualities in a true trinity. As

★'The Prayer of Azariah' and 'The Song of the Three Young Men' were
inserted between verses 23 and 24 of the third chapter of the Book of
Daniel.

the original text says, they began to sing 'as out of *one* mouth'.

The content of the song of praise is wonderfully ordered. It begins by looking at the Deity himself to whom the three had first turned in the fire:

> *Blessed art thou, O Lord, God of our fathers,*
>> *and to be praised and highly exalted for ever;*
> *And blessed is thy glorious, holy name:*
>> *and to be highly praised is thy glorious, holy name.*
> *Blessed art thou in the temple of thy holy glory,*
>> *and to be extolled and highly glorified for ever.*

To the Father-God is added the 'name' as something in its own right — as if it were a divination of the mystery of the Son born in eternity, in whom the Father reveals his being. Then thirdly the temple of glory, subsisting as it were in revealing light — here one could think of the sphere of the Holy Spirit.

In the three following verses there is a gradual descent from the innermost divine sphere of God towards *the world:* 'Blessed art thou, who sittest upon the cherubim and lookest upon the deeps . . .' There follows the picture of the 'throne' and finally the 'firmament'.

Up to this point the deity has been directly addressed: 'Thou' — 'Blessed art thou . . .' After something like a lower boundary of the highest divine regions is reached, the hymn turns to direct personal address to the 'works of the Lord'.

> *Bless the Lord, all works of the Lord,*
>> *sing praise to him and highly exalt him for ever.*

This verse structure with its threefold 'bless — praise — exalt' is maintained unchanged from now on. It is repeated unremittingly through no less than thirty-two double verses with the magnificent monotony of waves beating on the sea-shore.

Although the 'firmament' has been the demarcation of the lower reaches of the most holy regions, the upper regions of the earthly world now under review are nevertheless seen as its immediate 'neighbours', and closely connected with the divine. So when attention is turned to *the heavens above*, the song calls in order upon the 'heavens', the 'angels', the 'waters above the heaven', the 'powers' of the Lord, and in addition 'sun and moon' and the 'stars of heaven'. These shining phenomena are therefore regarded as no other than the lowest of the vast invisible world of the spirit that simply as it were 'hangs down' into the visible in the stars.

From the world of the upper heavens the hymn descends to what in a more limited sense can still be called 'the heavens', to the *atmosphere*, which mediates the transition from heaven to earth. In this realm the hymn even lingers with particularly loving minuteness of detail: 'all rain and dew', 'all winds', 'fire and heat', 'winter cold and summer heat', 'dews and snows', 'nights and days', 'light and darkness', 'ice and cold', 'frosts and snows', 'lightnings and clouds'.

Now for the first time, after lingering long over the wonders of the elemental processes of the atmosphere, the hymn 'lands' in the realm of earth. The *earth* as such is now therefore called upon as a special and manifoldly organized sphere of existence. Since the hymn moves from above to below, the earth is first set foot upon in its towering peaks, which are still in the neighbourhood of the heavens. 'Mountains and hills'. First the barren rocks. Then begins the vegetation. 'All things that grow on the earth'. Plant life leads to a consideration of the waters of the earth: 'springs', 'seas and rivers'.

From the plant kingdom the step is made to that of the animals. This began in the water. Moses' story of creation describes how at first animal existence teemed in the water, how next the air was conquered, and how finally the animal made its home on dry land. In the same order the hymn names 'whales and all creatures that move in the waters', 'all birds of the air', 'beasts and cattle'.

So the kingdoms of the creation are gone through. The phenomena of the world are looked at with the exalted feeling that comes from the experience of the fire. One could call it a kind of 'initiation'. Rudolf Steiner describes in his book, *Christianity as Mystical Fact*, the experience through which an initiate goes. 'He makes the journey to Hades. It is well for him if he does not now succumb — when a new world opens before him. Either he shrinks to nothing there, or he stands as one newly transformed before it. In the latter case a new sun and a new earth lie before him. Out of the spiritual fire the whole world is born for him again.' A world born out of the spiritual fire, a new sun, a new earth — that is also the content of the vision of the cosmos in the song of praise of the three in the furnace.

Why should the world arise anew for them out of the spiritual fire? Because they had found rebirth in themselves. Thus the great review of the world ends with *man*. Seven different calls to praise God go forth to the kingdom of man. They begin with the call to the 'sons of men', which indicates the future development of humanity beyond that time. Next 'Israel', prototype of the holy people, by Christians justly understood as prototype of the 'Church'. Then 'priests of the Lord' — 'servants of the Lord'. As priestly mediators between above and below men fulfil the task allotted them by their position between angel and beast. Thus they become servants of God. In fifth place comes the significant expression, 'spirits and souls of the righteous'. Man is not only body and soul, but as the image of the triune God he is also threefold: body, soul and spirit. Whoever in the best sense is 'a righteous man', putting himself in harmony with God and the world, is also bound to be able to live as spirit amongst spirits in the light-filled, all-embracing spiritual world. To the 'spirits and souls of the righteous' are added those 'who are holy and humble in heart'. In the seventh and last place there finally come the three singers of the hymn themselves. And not with their foreign Babylonian names that had been forced upon them in exile and with which they otherwise appear in the story of Daniel, but with their own original Hebrew names:

Bless the Lord, Hananiah, Azariah, and Mishael,
sing praise to him and highly exalt him for ever.

Thus the hymn concludes with those from whom it sprang. The three who went through the great fire experience how they inwardly reach a higher stage and consciously grasp the transformation that has come about in them. They have seen the world as reborn out of the fire, of the spirit. Now they recognize themselves as men new born out of that fire. There follow the words: 'For he has rescued us from Hades, and saved us from the hand of death.' It is like an Old Testament divination of the great mystery that first in full reality entered the world of men in Christ — the mystery of death and resurrection.

11. Leviathan. The dragon myth in the Old Testament

Every autumn after the full light of summer the soul senses the renewed encroachment of darkness. It is confronted by the picture — formed as it were out of the deepening darkness — of the dragon, that most ancient of human nightmares, prototype of man's fear and horror when faced with the powers opposed to God. Out of the all-pervading darkness the soul sees the dragon arise; out of the refined spiritual light with which a supersensory sun irradiates this autumn darkening there takes shape before it the picture of one who conquers the dragon.

It is very ancient human experience that stirs in the soul when it beholds the dragon and its conqueror. This vision, however, has its proper place in the present age only if the old picture is seen in the light of Christ's deed — as it is in the last book of the New Testament, the Revelation of John. There in the twelfth chapter the picture of the fight with the dragon is placed within the framework of Christian apocalypse, and is thus recognizable for the first time in its full significance.

The Bible is an organic whole. This is apparent when we see how the climax of apocalyptic imagery at the end of the New Testament — Michael's fight with the dragon — is not unprepared for, but already has its first elements in the Old Testament.

The dragon-myth in the Old Testament? Is not the Old Testament really *un*mythological in approach? This objection would not be without foundation. Consider for example the creation of the world. Moses' Genesis describes it in a manner appropriate to a people who were to be guided from a fading dreamlike picture consciousness to clear thinking. In comparison with the creation stories of other peoples, mythological imagery recedes markedly in favour of a more intellectual element. The power of thinking draws clear boundaries and distinguishes for the first time between world phenomena; we see at work in the creation story of Genesis something like a divine, cosmically active thinking; it masters uncontrolled chaos and 'thinks asunder' the various elements of the universe so that an ordered cosmos can arise. Thus God divides light and darkness, calls the one 'day' and the other 'night'. Thus he divides the water above from the water below, the firm land from the waters.

Apart, however, from the Mosaic story of creation into which there plays such a conspicuous element of thought, other different kinds of description of the origin of the world were obviously prevalent, genuinely 'pagan' in their mythological colouring and imagery, akin to certain Babylonian traditions.

While in Genesis we are presented so to speak with the 'official' line of Old Testament spirituality, we find the old mythology chiefly in the more *poetic* writings, not indeed as complete pictures, but in fragments from which something can be reconstructed. Traces of a long-past picture consciousness, dimmed by the approach of reasoned thought, turn up where the prevailing more abstract spirituality is temporarily relaxed — that is to say, in poetry. Here the old imaginative wealth often survives and radiates its mysterious soul-warming power even where, as being 'only poetic', it is not taken absolutely seriously.

Such 'erratics', remnants of a mythical consciousness, are found chiefly in the Book of Job, which seems to be remembered only for the wonderful saying about the world's beginning, 'when the morning stars sang together'. We have, then, in the first place to deal with the Book of Job if we want to pursue the dragon myth. Such research

89

into the mythical has its special attraction and value in our time when people want to reach beyond a merely intellectual consciousness to the sphere of imaginative vision.

Two monsters, Leviathan and Behemoth, are described at the end of the book. The explanatory footnotes added for example in the RSV are typical of an intellectual understanding of mythical imagery. These invite the reader to envisage a hippopotamus under the name of Behemoth and a crocodile under the name of Leviathan. He is thus rendered immune to any mythological thrill of horror, he feels at ease, and above all is left with the impression of how inaccurately nature was observed in those ancient, unenlightened times. He then takes this chapter as a rather inexact poetical fantasy about animals that one can nowadays view at leisure in the zoo — where one certainly never sees a crocodile spitting fire, as Job describes Leviathan:

> His sneezings flash forth light,
>> and his eyes are like the eyelids of the dawn.
> Out of his mouth go flaming torches;
>> sparks of fire leap forth.
> Out of his nostrils comes forth smoke,
>> as from a boiling pot and burning rushes.
> His breath kindles coals,
>> and a flame comes forth from his mouth.   (Job 41:18–21)

Leviathan — a crocodile? Rather the other way round: the crocodile — a Leviathan! In other words the crocodile, like the ancient saurians before it, still calls up a remote reminiscence of the dragon. Faced by the terrifying form of the crocodile the sensitive soul still feels something of the dragon-fear of ancient times. Granted that in Job's time nature could not yet be observed accurately. That is undoubted. But perhaps certain 'inaccuracies' of ancient story-tellers should be explained by a resurgence of ancient clairvoyance which was then unconsciously woven into the physical observation. The sight of the crocodile could trigger off 'second sight' of the dragon, and the mythical vision settled like a cloud in front of what the physical eyes saw. Thus this passage taken as a description of a crocodile may be rated inaccurate throughout; nevertheless, as a vision of evil it is more firmly based in reality than a superficial zoological catalogue. It is the Lucifer qualities of the dragon that spit out at us from the description in Job, which ends with the words: 'He is king over all the sons of pride.'

The Book of Job does not speak of dragons only in Chapters 40 and 41. It already mentions them earlier in reference to a myth that it assumes to be well known. In this case, though, the dragon is not called Leviathan but 'Rahab', in view of his terrible ferocity. As in Babylonian myth the helpers of the monster are mentioned.

The story is concerned with an event at the beginning of time. The universe would not have become an ordered cosmos if the God of the 'I am' had not put the forces of chaos in their place and wrested the world order from them.

> *He is God; no one can stay his anger;*
> *beneath him had to bow the helpers of Rahab.*
> *(Job 9:13. Author's translation)*

The same struggle is spoken of later:

> *By his power he stilled the sea;*
> *by his understanding he smote Rahab.*
> *By his wind the heavens were made fair;*
> *his hand pierced the fleeing serpent.   (26:12–13)*

The God of the 'I am'[*] is at the same time the God of the power of thinking who, creating clarity, conquered chaos. By his 'understanding' he struck down Rahab. Cleansing the atmosphere, which in the ancient days of dragons was a seething vapour, making possible a clear heaven and a pure, spirit-bearing breeze (in Hebrew as in Greek the same word indicates both 'air' and 'spirit') — these are the

---

[*]Hermann Beckh once freely rendered 'Yahweh': 'He who speaks the "I" in me'.

consequences of the primeval victory of Yahweh over the dragon, preparations in the natural world for the appearance of man the thinker.

The Psalms also tell of this myth (89:9f);

> *Thou dost rule the raging of the sea;*
> *when its waves rise, thou stillest them.*
> *Thou didst crush Rahab like a carcass . . .*

Similarly in Psalm 74 (13f) the raging sea is the element of the dragon, whose fearful, multi-headed image emerges from the waters as in the Apocalypse:

> *Thou didst divine the sea by thy might;*
> *thou didst break the heads of the dragons on the waters.*
> *Thou didst crush the heads of Leviathan,*
> *thou didst give him as food for the people of [in] the wilderness.* ★

The latter passage recalls the far-reaching prophecy of apocryphal tradition that one day at the end of time Leviathan is to serve as food for the chosen people — the enormous energy active in the ungodly is one day to be won back to the good, 'incorporated' in those associated with God. So something of the future shines into this remarkable sentence about the approaching feeding of the people in the wilderness, whilst it also refers back to a long past event. The singer of Psalm 74, who has had to experience the destruction of the Temple, faces the question: How is it that the Adversary apparently seizes the earth? Then he remembers the great conquest of the dragon in the dim past and is bound to ask himself: Where is this power of conquest today? He cannot yet perceive that this power is undergoing a lengthy process of transformation, that in the future it will conquer the dragon in man, and by means of man himself.

The same question — in modern words, 'Is God dead?' — troubled the soul of the prophet Isaiah (51:9):

★RSV alternative reading, following the Hebrew text. The author would read 'in' rather than 'of'.

Awake, awake, put on strength,
  O arm of the LORD;
awake, as in days of old,
  the generations of long ago.
Was it not thou that didst cut Rahab in pieces,
  that didst pierce the dragon?

This power once conquered the dragon, but the fight brought no final decision. The dragon is 'wounded' but not dead.

This is recalled in a story from the Edda about the fight by Thor against the Midgard snake. Thor rows out to sea with the giant Hymir. He uses the head of a black bull for bait. The Midgard snake bites, Thor draws it up and as its frightful head emerges from the sea he hurls his hammer — but the blow does not strike with fatal impact; at the last moment Hymir has treacherously cut the line. The stricken monster sinks, but now there is the uncertainty whether it is dead or still alive. Will it recover? Will another fight be necessary?

The myth of which traces are found in the Old Testament also shows an awareness that the dragon conquered in primeval times now lives hidden in the sea. This is clear from the book of the prophet Amos (9:3): 'and though they hide from my sight at the bottom of the sea, there I will command the serpent, and it shall bite them.'

The serpent lurks at the bottom of the sea. A mysterious passage in Job shows that this does not only concern the outer world; it makes it clear how such myths are relevant to the inner life. The sea is at the same time the soul. And as in the sea there are the so-called 'abyssal' deeps into which no ray of sunlight falls, in whose unlit, black darkness a most sinister and fearful world of creatures has its existence (one thinks of the pictures deep sea exploration has given us), so there are also the unillumined abyssal depths of the soul-sea, in which fiendish and terrible monsters hide. They will not always remain 'latent' — the visionary John sees the future rising of the beast from the abyss (Rev. 17:8) for a final conflict with the powers of light.

In the world past, the dragon was conquered; in the world present, it is 'latent' in sinister, threatening manner. What yet sleeps in the abysses of the soul can become awake. Schiller described how the magic of song penetrates into the deeper levels of the soul and stirs them: 'And wakes the hidden power of feeling so wonderfully sleeping in the heart.' There the poet thinks of what is great and noble sleeping in the heart and waiting to be woken. But evil in its most terrible form is also still hidden. To awaken and call up these forces is a deed of black magic.

It is of this that Job speaks in the very obscure passage already mentioned. In his despair he would curse the day of his birth. But it is clear to him as a man of ancient times that if it is to work, the curse like the blessing is determined by certain soul conditions and has to be skilled. Just as a momentary flaring up of good will is not enough to be able to bless effectively, so a fit of anger has not the power of effective cursing. When now even the day of his birth is to be cursed, Job accordingly looks out as it were for someone who is skilled in cursing. Then a dark and sinister picture of earlier times arises in his darkened soul: the black magicians of submerged Atlantis.

Herodotus in one place writes about the Atlanteans, who were so wicked that every day they cursed the rising sun. One could imagine no more apt characterization of black magic than this curse hurled against the sun every morning.

The passage in Job runs: 'Let those curse it [the night of his conception] who curse the day, who are skilled to rouse up Leviathan' (Job 3:8). Here Greek and Hebrew tradition coincide. Those 'who curse the day' are the wicked Atlanteans of Herodotus, those who so vehemently hate the rising sun. They set themselves against the Christ principle of the sunlit day, which by grace illumines the meaning of earth existence. They are there when it comes to cursing human birth on earth. They are therefore also able to 'rouse up Leviathan' — to call up and awaken what sleeps dragon-like in the 'abyssal' bottom of the soul's sea.

It is characteristic of the marvellous contrapuntal style of the Bible that before the rising of the Christ-Day ('I am the light of the world . . . Abraham rejoiced that he was to see my day; he saw it and was glad', John 8:12, 56) a soul seeking God has to probe these abysses of negation.

What is hidden will come to light; the beast will rise from the abyss. 'The sun brings everything to light.' Once again Michael will gain the victory over the dragon in a new way in the future. Isaiah prophesies it (27:1):

> In that day the LORD with his hard and great and strong sword will punish Leviathan the fleeing serpent, Leviathan the twisting serpent, and he will slay the dragon that is in the sea.

But it will not be possible for this apocalyptic battle to be waged apart from man and without his involvement, like the earlier one. That battle could not be concluded since it was only to secure for man the natural foundations of his human existence intended for him at the creation. Indeed we already get in the Old Testament a distant hint of this future involvement of mankind. Man in association with the angels is to triumph over the dragon:

> For he will give his angels charge of you
>   to guard you in all your ways.
> On their hands they will bear you up,
>   lest you dash your foot against a stone.
> You will tread on the lion and the adder,
>   the young lion and the serpent you will trample under
>   foot.   (Ps.91:11–13)

These are words that play a very significant part in the New Testament.*

By regaining through Christ his connection with angelic realms above, man will be a match for the dragon. He finds

*See p. 77, Psalm 91.

his strength by looking up to the starry heights of hi
heavenly origin. This makes possible the glorious appear
ance at the end of the New Testament of John's mighty
vision of Michael's fight with the dragon — a primeva
picture, but one that now proclaims something entirely
new — a future of man with Christ.

12. 'Not by might . . .' The kingship of the Messiah

Mankind was prepared for the coming of Christ in manifold ways. As part of this preparation there developed in the world of the Old Covenant two complementary 'ideals' that served to direct awareness to the One expected. They were those of 'king' and 'priest' — the one concerned with the world, ruling with enlightenment, the other tending the connection with the heavens.

At the very beginning of Israelitic development proper there appears the mystery-shrouded picture of Melchizedek, a king of peace who is at the same time priest of the Most High God. He represents the ideal blending of king and priest.

More than half a millennium after Melchizedek, in the time of Moses, the people of the Old Covenant saw the founding of a special priesthood, with Aaron as the first high priest. A few hundred years later a first king was anointed. In Saul and Samuel, king and high priest appear together for the first time side by side. One can then observe how after that the two lines move apart, how they occasionally meet again, how antagonism arises between them, but also fruitful tension that prepares the possibility of a merging of a higher kind in the future.

The word 'Christ', Greek *christós*, is originally the translation of the Hebrew 'Messiah' (*mashiach*): the anointed one. Both the king and the high priest* were anointed. Each can be called 'the anointed of the LORD'. Philo, the Jewish sage

---

*Only the high priests, not the others, were consecrated by having their heads anointed with oil (Lev.8:12,30). In Lev.4:3, the 'anointed priest' means 'high priest'.

living in Alexandria, saw in the high priest the representative of the divine Logos. But every king too who bore the crown in Jerusalem as 'son of David' was felt to be holding the position of the greater One who was to come. In itself a prophecy, the series of royal sons of David following each other through the centuries seemed like the keeping alive of a permanently burning holy light.★ In the eyes of the Jew the king could from time to time already come very close to what he was meant only to foreshadow. In Psalm 45, which celebrates a royal marriage, the princely bridegroom is already seen as almost indistinguishable from his divine prototype. Later on, moreover, the rabbis thought that the Messiah should have been recognized as actually already present in King Hezekiah.

In the New Testament the evangelist Matthew has a special eye for how the long-prepared line of 'images' of the king moves towards the figure of Christ Jesus and finds its fulfilment in him. He begins his account with a genealogy in which — different from Luke — he expressly adds to the name David, 'the king' (Matt. 1:6) and — again different from Luke — follows the ancestry of Jesus from David through Solomon and thence through the whole succession of kings who ruled in Jerusalem. These form the middle of the three groups into which Matthew subdivides his genealogical tree. The series of kings reaches up to the catastrophe of the destruction of Jerusalem in 586. Then the Babylonians brought the Jewish kings to a terrible end, burnt the Temple and led the people into exile. From that point Matthew lists the third group of his genealogy, which leads to Jesus.

In this connection Emil Bock pointed out that those belonging to this third group certainly lived on in the minds of the Jews as the 'uncrowned kings'. Near the beginning of this list appears one who represents an important turning

★ 1Kings 11:36; 15:4; 2Kings 8:19 (also 2Chron. 21:7); Psalm 132:17.

point in the history of the Old Testament idea of the king — that is Zerubbabel.

We imagine ourselves back in the year 520 BC. Eighteen years have passed since the Persian king, Cyrus, overthrew the kingdom of Babylon and gave the deported Jews permission to return home to Jerusalem and rebuild the Temple. Since this return they have gradually re-established themselves in the ruined city, to some extent already even quite comfortably — one stern prophet points out the wood-panelled houses that people have already acquired, while the Temple is still not rebuilt. Those who have returned look to two leading men who since 538 have energetically taken the fate of the people in hand. The one is Zerubbabel, 'son of David'. The Persians have made him governor. Special hopes, however, are concentrated on him. He is the present 'uncrowned king' and it is believed he will re-establish the monarchy. Beside him stands the high priest who bears the name of salvation — Joshua. In the Greek tongue this name is 'Jesus'.

As Providence placed these two figures like prototypes, so it now also calls up a further pair to give a spiritual impulse, two 'prophets'. First appears Haggai in the autumn of 520. He it is who reproaches the people for dwelling in warm, comfortable new houses and appeals to their consciences about the rebuilding of the Temple, which is still not done. With words that are also relevant to our own age he depicts how unsatisfactory it is to strive only for material well-being, how that must finally leave the soul empty if the Temple is not also rebuilt, the connection with the divine cared for. 'You have sown much, and harvested little; you eat, but you never have enough; you drink, but you never have your fill; you clothe yourselves, but no one is warm; and he who earns wages earns wages to put them into a bag with holes' (Hagg. 1:6). In exemplary manner this sentence captures the suffering from an unfulfilled existence that we Europeans call 'frustration'. The prophet calls the people away from this egoistical waste of energy in striving for material well-being and injects into their souls the burning impulse for building the Temple. He turns in the first place to the two leading men: to Zerubbabel and Joshua. His appeal catches fire. 'And the LORD stirred up the spirit of Zerubbabel . . . and the spirit of Joshua . . . the high priest, and the spirit of all the remnant of the people' so that in the middle of September the building is begun (1:14f). At the beginning of October, also in the season of Michael, prophecy goes a step further.

Haggai's utterances become apocalyptic. Coming world-shaking events seek to find expression through him. 'For thus says the LORD of hosts: Once again, in a little while, I will shake the heavens and the earth . . .' (2:6). Beyond this shaking shines final fulfilment. The LORD will dwell in this Temple, in Jerusalem. 'And in this place I will give peace' (2:9 AV).

We notice here a peculiarity common to consciousness reaching into the supersensory: it is clearly not altogether easy for the seer to observe accurately *when* the event he 'sees coming' will be, how near or far off this coming is. Once in the time of Moses the seer Baalam could observe of the star his vision had revealed: 'I see him, but not now; I behold him, but not nigh' (Num.24:17). Haggai in 520 already belongs to a very much later time when the original, more instinctive faculty of supersensory vision has become something stranger. So the 'but not now . . . but not nigh' escapes him. Since Baalam, it is true, eight hundred years had elapsed, but there were still to be five hundred years till the coming of Christ; and the last 'shaking of heaven and earth' that entered his clairvoyant field of vision still today belongs to the future, though it is again and again heralded by catastrophes running ahead of it.

We could well imagine that at the fateful time of the rebuilding of the Temple the future flashed forth in the supersensory as if in a spiritual storm, so that what was still far off could seem near. The time perspective gets lost, it contracts into mighty close-ups what in fact will be a much longer lasting, much more complicated series of events. It is not therefore even really the second Temple built on earth under Zerubbabel and Joshua to which the promise applies; this temple simply stands for what in John's Gospel is called the 'temple of his body'. So we are not surprised, or doubtful of the genuineness of Haggai's inspiration, when we notice another 'short cut'. The prophet has arrived at the mystery of the Messiah. But his vision is caught up as it were by the figure of Zerubbabel who stands so close to him and is associated with so many hopes; it remains attached to this figure in the foreground. Thus it happens that Zerubbabel is proclaimed Messiah-King of God's future kingdom (2:21–23).

While Haggai looks first and foremost at Zerubbabel, the other of the two prophets, Zechariah, who became active somewhat later, shows a stronger interest in the high priest Joshua. To Zechariah also were vouchsafed Messianic and apocalyptic revelations. For him too the distinction between the Palestinian Jerusalem and the future city of God, the heavenly Jerusalem of the Apocalypse, is not yet altogether clear. Even through the pictures of the material world, however, there breaks the supersensory picture of the perfection he divines when he announces that the future Jerusalem no longer requires walls: the Lord himself encompasses it as a wall of fire, and within the fiery circle dwells the divine 'glory' (Zech. 2:5). Zechariah knows that God is already on his way toward dwelling within the human. 'Be silent, all flesh, before the LORD; for he has roused himself from his holy dwelling.' (2:13).

Then Zechariah has a divine vision (3:1) of the high priest, Joshua. He stands in a dirty garment before the angel of the Lord and has to suffer Satan's accusation. By a divine act of grace he has a clean new priest's robe bestowed on him. In other words his priesthood, sullied by the all too human way he has borne the office, is restored in the purity of its original form. At the same time, however, it becomes clear that this does not mean the final perfection. It will first be possible to speak of the immaculate high priest only when the other Joshua-Jesus has appeared. Joshua is therefore told he and his fellow priests are only 'men of good omen', and the true Messiah is mentioned immediately after, separate from their prefigurement of him.

The 'Branch' is spoken of — in Hebrew *ṣemach*, Latin *'oriens'*. The Greek word, *'anatolé'*, means both the coming up of a plant and the rising of a star. 'Behold', I will bring my servant the Branch' (3:8). Then immediately another image: God prepares a stone over which watch seven eyes, and which he says he will engrave with its inscription (3:9, where RSV translates 'facets' instead of 'eyes'). The seven eyes indicate the cosmic being of Christ, who uses the 'seven planets' as his eyes. The engraving on the stone is a wonderful image for the fact that by the divine Word's becoming flesh the Spirit intends to brings its influence right down into earthly matter and imprint itself there.

Zechariah's visions reach a climax in the fourth chapter. The prophet experiences the transition to supersensory vision as an awakening from deep sleep — so seems everyday consciousness in comparison, say, with an angel's. Being awoken he sees the golden lampstand with the seven lamps. The seven celestial lights want to find their abode on earth, and they become the seven lamps borne by the lampstand. This is also an image for the incarnation of the heavenly in the earthly. The sun quality of the Christ-being expresses itself in the golden sheen of the lampstand. But if the heavenly light is to appear on earth borne by a lampstand, it needs fuel; oil must flow to it so that the holy flame remains alive. Zechariah therefore sees to right and left of the golden lampstand the two olive trees as 'the two anointed who stand by the LORD of the whole earth' (4:14). The two anointed: they represent the kingly and the priestly elements which by serving the heavenly being of Christ contribute towards his appearance on earth.

Apparently very abruptly in the midst of all this, (and therefore suspected by critics of not belonging to this text), there now also appears in the Book of Zechariah — for the first time — the name of Zerubbabel. 'This is the word of the LORD to Zerubbabel: Not by might, nor by power, but by my Spirit . . .' (4:6). This is the decisive moment. With these words of God — the two negatives so emphatically setting aside the element of external power which had hitherto been inseparable from the image of king — the idea of Messiah-King is set free from that of earthly dominion. What is so clearly said 'about Zerubbabel' is also applicable to the other members of the third group in Matthew's genealogy that ends with Jesus. The 'uncrowned kings' are thus now no longer only potential kings impeded by the adverse circumstances of the time, but since Zerubbabel they represent a radically transformed and spiritualized idea of kingship. In a later chapter of the Book of Zechariah we then find the Palm Sunday lines about the gentle king who does not force the entrance as a conqueror, but allows his entry to depend on whether he is freely bidden welcome (9:9).

Zechariah is also not yet wholly free of the prejudice arising from a short-term view, speaking words in relation to Zerubbabel which obviously were not fulfilled (4:7–10). Here we notice a gap in the Old Testament record. After the enthusiastic and energetic commencement of the Temple building, the name of Zerubbabel disappears without trace from the texts. On the completion of the building — already achieved in March 516 — he is not named. Some tragedy must certainly be concealed behind this lack of mention. Perhaps an illness carried him off? We do not know.

The Book of Zechariah comes back once more to the other anointed one, to Joshua. At God's command Zechariah takes some of the gold and silver that pious Jews coming from Babylon have given for Jerusalem, and makes from it a crown (6:11). The plural 'crowns' in the original text perhaps indicates that it concerns a double crown, one part of silver and the other of gold. Already in Haggai we read: 'The silver is mine, and the gold is mine, says the LORD of hosts' (2:8). Silver and gold direct attention beyond their material metallic existence to the great cosmic forces that work in moon and sun. From silver and gold, therefore, a crown is shaped, and in a kind of visionary-symbolic act placed on the head of the high priest, Joshua. It is not a political act with political consequences. It is like a prophetic and sacred dream-play concerning the bearer of the name 'Jesus', the man 'of good omen'. It is like a prophecy that one day another Jesus will carry in him the sun-being of Christ that makes the moon forces subservient. The crown does not stay on the head of the high priest Joshua — for he is not yet the one who can finally unite in himself both king and priest. The crown is taken from his head again and henceforth kept in the Temple as a sacred token of the longed-for mystery. In direct connection with this Zechariah speaks for the second time of the 'Branch' that will one day 'grow up' (6:12).

Only Christ Jesus combines in the deepest sense sun-kingship with humble self-sacrifice. He is truly a king not 'in spite of' but 'because of' his offering of himself. When we sense the touch of his presence, then the old prophetic words of almost two and a half thousand years ago take on a new glory: 'Not by might, nor by power, but by my Spirit'.

TREE, WELLS, AND STONES IN THE LIVES OF THE PATRIARCHS

13. Abraham and the trees

The ancient peoples knew about sacred trees. They knew of meetings with the unseen world which had taken place under such trees and in consecrated groves. The picture-vision of Genesis sees Adam, not yet separated from God, walking under the trees of the garden of Eden.

An old and mighty tree is venerable and marvellous. Its roots reach deep down into the dark earth. Its lofty stem towers high in kingly pride. This upward striving being is not short-lived like the flame which darts up only to sink back into itself again; the tree stands steadfast and enduring. In it there is something of the long will of eternity. Decades and centuries have inscribed their circles inside its bark. This calm, steady, dependable being awakens trust, one puts faith in it. Its power to grow upward becomes a power to uphold. The branches spread on all sides, and form a vault over the piece of earth below. The tree's silent strength spreads over men's heads — a rustling, whispering heaven, in which the wind celebrates the mysteries of its secret, invisible being.

1 The oak at Shechem

Such an ancient holy tree is at the consecrated place of Shechem (which is later called Samaria). At the 'oak of Shechem' Abraham first stops in the promised land.

He has obeyed God's voice which has laid stern commands upon him. He has left behind him the temples of Ur and of Haran, the places of Chaldean wisdom of moon and stars. Now for the first time he treads the soil of the country which God has shown him, which is to become the scene of the events of Christ's life on earth.

Today we regard 'making a journey' purely from the practical point of view of getting from A to B; at most we might consider the traveller and the sights he is to see. But we could look at it from another point of view: what does it mean for the landscape that man walks through it. Not only does the visible, material part of a human being affect the surroundings, but the person's inner soul-spiritual being is connected through the fine ethereal life-forces to the whole of nature around him. There is an interplay between the invisible in man and in nature of which we are usually quite unaware. Goethe's words, 'the place a good man visits is hallowed,' are much truer than we might think at first. A landscape is affected by the people passing through it: something is left in the 'aura' of that area. Thus there are sanctuaries where the fine ethereal 'footprints' of a great and good person can still be felt in the invisible weaving of forces for a long time afterwards. There are also places which are cursed.

The Holy Land is already prepared for the coming of the Christ a long time before the event. Part of this preparation is the journeying of the patriarchs. The first who takes on this task of 'consecrating' the land is Abraham. His wanderings follow not only the necessities of a more or less nomadic existence, but follow divine command: 'Arise, walk through the length and the breadth of the land, for I will give it to you.' (13:17). His wanderings to the north and south, east and west describe a great cross which is spiritually impregnated into the land.

The way in which he walks there shows that his wanderings are determined by a hidden spiritual geography of the holy places. Conscious of his goal he passed on to Shechem without delay and made his first resting place in the promised land beside the ancient oak, which was already regarded as sacred by the Canaanites.

At this consecrated oak of Shechem he was permitted to behold God for the first time in the new land. In remembrance of it he built an altar there. The cult of sacrifice would henceforth maintain and foster a living union with the divinity which had there revealed itself. The Bible tells of other altars built by the patriarch, but it is not unimportant that this building of altars began under the oak of Shechem, or that this first place of sacrifice made by Abraham was blessed by a sacred tree.

> *When they had come to the land of Canaan, Abram passed through the land to the place at Shechem, to the oak of Moreh. At that time the Canaanites were in the land. Then the LORD appeared to Abram, and said, 'To your descendants I will give this land.' So he built there an altar to the LORD, who had appeared to him. (Gen.12:5–7).*

In Hebrew the word 'place' (*maqom*) has a special significance. It is not only a 'place' in the ordinary sense, but implies a special sanctuary. So 'the place at Shechem' is an ancient holy site. On closer research these ancient holy places are often found to have been special since time immemorial. Often the place of Christian pilgrimage was a heathen sanctuary. Such sites remain holy through the changes of time and religion. This can also be seen in the Bible. The holy places of the Israelites were Canaanite sanctuaries before, and were simply incorporated into the new religion. Abraham must have known of the sanctuary at Shechem when he came from Babylonia in the east and 'passed through the land to the place at Shechem, to the oak of Moreh' (12:6).

The oak of Moreh could be called 'the oak of the master-teacher'. In this name lies the memory of a wise man who perhaps dwelt beneath this oak long before Abraham's arrival. People must have come to this hermit to seek his wisdom. But we should not imagine that the place became holy through this sage. He will have been attracted to the place because it was special before. His presence will have added to its 'atmosphere'.

At this place Abraham stayed for a longer time. There he received his first divine revelation. The locality will have helped this experience, for a revelation can come closer to man in the fine atmosphere of a sanctuary. Abraham responds to the revelation by building an altar. In the offering cult the connection to the divine is maintained. True ritual is originally always connected with divine revelation; it has grown out of it, and it seeks to re-establish the relationship to the divine.

Later we hear again, in passing, of the sacred oak. When, at the divine command, Jacob begins to build an altar at Bethel, he first makes his followers purify themselves from the images of the heathen cults, and buries statues of the gods and heathen amulets under the oak of Shechem (Gen. 35:4).

Again, after the conquest of the promised land, when Joshua holds in Shechem a great assembly of the tribes, he knows of no worthier place for the stone pillar, which he sets up in remembrance of the renewal of the covenant, than 'under the oak in the sanctuary of the LORD' (Josh. 24:26).

The decadence of the Canaanite religion brought with it all kinds of magical arts. These were practised at this sacred place, and the tree of Shechem became known as the 'magic oak' (Judg. 9:37, author's translation).

2 *The grove of Mamre*

When he returned from his journey to Egypt Abraham chose as his dwelling place for a considerable time the oak-grove of Mamre by Hebron.

This grove also had been previously discovered by

Abraham to be an ancient holy place. The Jewish writer Josephus, who lived in the first Christian century, tells of an oak of Ogyges which was pointed out there. Ogyges — this name points back into mythical ages. Phoenician tradition speaks of a mythical king of the Titans who bore this name. This connection is also indicated by the other name which Hebron bore, Kiriath-arba, the town of Arba (Gen. 23:2). Arba was said to have been the ancestor of the Titans. Thus this place is haunted by secrets of past races of giants, who did not yet feel themselves to be limited and enclosed by the skin of the compact, earthly, human body.

Mamre, the owner of the grove of like name, must have been a kind of guardian of this place of the mysteries. He was obviously the leader among three brothers (Mamre, Eshcol, and Aner). With these three brothers Abraham made an alliance (Gen. 14:13).

This taking up of his abode in the grove of Mamre was no casual event. Abraham built there an altar. That was done only in consecrated places, 'So Abraham . . . dwelt by the oaks of Mamre, which are at Hebron, and there he built an altar to the LORD.' (Gen. 13:18).

One of the most solemn events in Abraham's life was his meeting with Melchizedek, the priest-king of Salem, who gave him bread and wine, thus prophesying the institution of the Lord's Supper. So there fell upon the patriarch a ray from Christ's kingdom of the sun which was now drawing near (Compare Heb. 7:3). That this event occurs during Abraham's stay in Mamre is not without significance; for the place where one meets an important event is always significant, as is the place to which one goes after the event, when the soul is still filled with the experience. An experience needs a preparation for it, then, after it has occurred, it leaves its echo behind and works itself out to its fulfilment. The place where Abraham experienced the preparation for and the sequel of this visit of Melchizedek was the grove of Mamre.

Following the meeting with Melchizedek there are three significant revelations of God to Abraham during his fourteen years at Mamre. The first, while he was still under the influence of this visit to Melchizedek, was when Abraham had the wonderful revelation of the stars. God himself, 'brought him outside' and showed him the stars (Gen. 15:5). One sees many things, and yet never really 'sees' them until they are shown. Such a 'showing,' which opened the eyes and awakened them to see visions, was the especial duty of the priest who dedicated the pupil in the old mysteries. Here the Godhead itself is the 'mystagogue' who leads his pupil on to vision. 'He brought him outside', is a saying which in its mysterious matter-of-factness and simplicity is equal to that other which says that God himself shut the door of the ark behind Noah, (Gen. 7:16). He led Abraham 'out'. He took him outside the four walls of narrow everyday life; he removed the constraint of a consciousness which was merely earthly and said, 'Look toward heaven.' In the glory of the starry heavens which God showed him the patriarch received the promise of posterity. Overarched by the vault of heaven, he felt in his heart the power of faith. 'And he believed in the LORD' (Gen. 15:6 AV).

His sojourn in the grove of Mamre may well have helped the soul of Abraham to grow ripe for this revelation of the stars.

The cosmos sometimes appeared to men of ancient times in the vision of the mighty tree of the gods, in whose boughs the shining stars hung, like golden fruit. That which heaven did in large, they saw the tree do in image and parable as it overshadowed the earth with its vaulted branches and blessed it. As the cosmos is in the organism of streaming life, so also is the tree, which draws the sap of life into its most delicate branches. As the divine breath of the spirit breathes throughout the cosmos, so does the whispering wind blow through the leaves of the tree.

Although it is not expressly mentioned, yet, by the whole

context, we are led to conclude that the grove of Mamre is the place where in the second great revelation Abraham received the promise of a son, Isaac. There the rite of circumcision was performed, and his new, changed name was given him. Abram and Sarai are henceforth called Abraham and Sarah. In both cases, the name is enriched by the addition of the same sound, the 'h', the consonant which is furthest from earth and nearest to heaven. It is the sound of the breath. Under the rustling of the trees of Mamre this breath of the blowing wind, of the spirit's breathing, enters by inspiration into both names.

But the third revelation given at Mamre reaches the highest point with the divine apparition in the form of the three men who sit at table with Abraham. The divine Trinity has come to him as guest. They appear to him in his ninety-ninth year to proclaim the birth of Isaac. It can hardly be a coincidence that the divine Trinity is revealed to the lonely old man at that point in his life when he is on the threshold of an experience of 'the son'. This revelation allows us to sense the mystery that God is not the 'alone', the 'all-one', but that the Tri-une is 'I' and 'we' at once. The birth of Isaac is the precondition for the patriarchal trinity of Abraham, Isaac, and Jacob. This threefoldness is a clear image of the Trinity which is only fully revealed in the coming of Christ.

The objection could be raised that it was not really the Trinity, but 'the LORD' and two angels. After the meal Abraham accompanies them for a short distance and then 'the LORD' remains with Abraham while the two others go on to Sodom. However, a careful perusal of the text does not give the impression that two of the three are servants, though they are not always acting together: sometimes it is only 'the LORD'. Textual criticism sees the careless editing of two different sources. Before examining such a hypothesis, let us look at the text. We see a rhythmic alternation between the singular and the plural:

Singular	*Plural*
And the LORD appeared to him (18:1)	
	. . . and behold, three men stood . . . Abraham ran . . . to meet them (18:2)
'My lord, if I have found favour in your [thy] sight . . . (18:3)	
	Let a little water be brought and wash your [plural] feet, and rest yourselves under the tree . . .'
	. . . and he stood by them under the tree while they ate.
	They said to him . . . (18:4–9)
The LORD said, 'I will surely return to you in the spring, and Sarah your wife shall have a son.' . . . He [the LORD] said, 'No, but you did laugh.' (18:10–15)	
	Then the men set out from there, . . . (18:16)
The LORD said, 'Shall I hide from Abraham what I am about to do . . .' (18:17–21)	
	So the men turned from there, and went toward Sodom; (18:22a)
but Abraham still stood before the LORD.★ . . . (18:22b–33)	

★'The men turned from there' does not imply only two. The LORD himself says, 'I will go down to see . . .'. It is as if the three depart together. When it goes on to say 'but Abraham stood before the LORD',

We have the impression of a breathing in and breathing out in the one, the three, the one . . . in three times three parts. A breathing of the mystery of the three-in-one.

Into this tale, the motif of the tree is significantly woven. Not only does it begin by saying: 'And the LORD appeared to him by the oaks of Mamre,' (18:1) but in the course of the story we find this emphasized. Abraham says to his guests, 'rest yourselves under the tree,' (18:4), 'he stood by them under the tree while they ate.' (18:8).

The ancient tree spread its holy shade over the divine meal.

3 The tree-planting in Beer-sheba

But Isaac was not born in Hebron. Before his birth Abraham left the grove of Mamre and went into the land of the Philistines, to the place which was to be specially connected in future with his son Isaac: Beer-sheba, the city of the well. As Hebron and the grove of Mamre is Abraham's town, so Beer-sheba is the town of Isaac.

A symbolic event lets us see very clearly that in entering Beer-sheba Abraham entered the future world, the world of the son.

Abraham planted a tamarisk tree in Beer-sheba, and called there on the name of the LORD, the Everlasting God' (21:33).

Until then we see Abraham under ancient trees; now in the city of his son, he plants a young tree. The Jews went even so far as to place Abraham's tree as a tree of healing beside the tree of paradise where man fell into sin. * 'The wise men say that because Adam ate of the Tree of Knowledge, he brought death into the world. But when Abraham came,

we must not forget that the whole description is a revelation, and these imaginative events do not obey the pragmatic logic of the everyday world. It may be that Abraham 'saw' the departure of the three and subsequently 'spoke' with the 'one'.

*Gorion, Sagen der Juden, 2.273.

he healed the world again by another tree.' One may say this is in all truth only of the cross of the Redeemer. Of him alone that true which is said about the tree of Beer-sheba. The Jewish sages regarded as fulfilment what was only prophecy. But in so far as it was true prophecy, they came near to attaining deep knowledge. The young tree of new healing was planted in the city of the son, in Beer-sheba. This son is a preconfiguration of the eternal Son who brings again to men the power of the Tree of Life in order to heal them. Abraham's offering of Isaac upon Mount Moriah is an annunciation of Golgotha, as Christendom has always understood. Beer-sheba is the place of preparation for the offering up of Isaac and the place where its immediate effect was felt. From Beer-sheba, Abraham and Isaac went out to Moriah, and to Beer-sheba they immediately afterwards returned. So the planting of the tree is a prophecy of the Tree of Life, which by the sacrifice of the Son shall grow green for the healing of the world. Abraham is sometimes called a prophet (20:7); however, his prophecy does not lie in words, but in his actions.

After this prophetic entry into the sphere of the Son, Abraham returns into his own world. He passes the last decades of his long patriarchal life in the grove of Mamre. There Sarah dies. There Abraham also dies. Their grave is the cave of Machpelah which Abraham had brought from the Hittites, with the piece of ground belonging to it and 'all the trees that were in the field' (23:17).

14. Isaac and the wells

We have found that Abraham's real place of abode was the grove of Mamre, near Hebron. But Isaac's abode is Beer-sheba, the city of wells. 'Beer' means 'well'. Beer-sheba means both 'seven wells' and 'the well of the oath'.

1 Beer-sheba

After the birth of Isaac Abraham dwelt for a time in Beer-sheba where he had planted the tree. In so doing he came out of his own sphere of life and symbolically entered, as a prophet, the sphere of his son.

Just as the meeting with Melchizedek was enclosed by Abraham's stay in Mamre, so the progress to Moriah and the sacrifice of Isaac was enclosed by his stay in Beer-sheba. There in the night he received the call to sacrifice; there afterwards the experience continued its influence upon him. 'So Abraham returned to his young men, and they arose and went together to Beer-sheba; and Abraham dwelt at Beer-sheba' (Gen. 22:19).

A remarkable scene precedes the events on Moriah. Abraham makes a compact with Abimelech, king of the Philistines. There has been a quarrel over the well at Beer-sheba. Abraham wishes to prove that this well had been dug by him. He therefore sets apart seven ewe lambs and gives them to the king in confirmation of his oath. Incidentally, this is the only story of a well which is told of Abraham in Genesis and it takes place in the town which may in a special sense be called the town of his son, Isaac. And, as the trees have a special significance for Abraham, so the wells have

for Isaac. The delicate attention paid to details in the compo-
sition of Genesis is shown by this placing of the picture of
the seven lambs immediately before the sacrifice of Isaac.
As in a solemn ritual the words 'seven lambs' are impressed
three times upon the ears of hearers.

> *Abraham set seven ewe lambs of the flock apart. And Abime-*
> *lech said to Abraham, 'What is the meaning of these seven ewe*
> *lambs which you have set apart?' He said, 'These seven ewe*
> *lambs you will take from my hand, that you may be a witness*
> *for me that I dug this well.' (22:28–30).*

The New Testament gives the key to these hieroglyphics
and shows the sublimity of these old pictures. Providence
formed objective prophecies of Christ, which were far
beyond the perceptions of those who took a part in them.
The seven lambs at Beer-sheba are like a prophecy of the
sevenfold powers of the Lamb of God, as they are seen (in
a changed picture) in the Apocalypse of John (5:6).

Between this picture of the seven lambs and the sacrifice
of Isaac, we find in its right place the story of the planting
of the young tree in Beer-sheba. 'Abraham planted a tamarisk tree in Beer-sheba, and called there on the name of the
LORD, the Everlasting God' (Gen. 31:33). This is a solemn
calling upon the name of God in a celebration of the cult.

It is here that we find the Everlasting God, or God of
Eternity, El-Olam. Genesis shows us how at that time
different aspects of the Godhead were perceived at different
holy places. The attributes of God which can be found
tabulated now in a primer of dogmatics as a series of
more or less abstract concepts were in earlier times living
experiences. At each holy place the hidden godhead revealed
another side of his nature to the pious worshippers. And so
every name which was given to the godhead had 'local
colour', the colour of the consecrated place. Thus at the
'well of him who lives and sees' they met El-Roi, the God
of seeing (Gen. 16:13). At Jerusalem El-Elyon, the 'Most
High God', was revealed by Melchizedek (19:18ff). In

Bethel El-Bethel, the 'God of Bethel', was revered, the God who will build his House of God upon earth (35:7).

This city of wells, Beer-sheba, with its young tree, gives to this name of God the 'local colour' of a concrete experience far removed from any abstraction. In the green of the young tree the God who renews the world reveals his power to rejuvenate. This is he who in the power of his eternity brings on the new 'for ever', the new aeon, the new cycle of time; who also, out of the divine wells that are never dry, draws 'the re-enlivening of the dying earth-existence'.★ 'El-Olam': the name throws its radiance over the chapter which immediately follows that of the sacrifice on Mount Moriah. One might also say: This name of God reveals in what follows even greater depths of its own mystery. The God who reveals his eternity in the cycle of time is the God of death and resurrection.

The offering of Isaac is the most sublime of the prophecies of the sacrifice of Christ contained in the Old Testament. In the Epistle to the Romans Paul cites the word of God which was spoken on Mount Moriah in order to express the mystery of the Father 'who did not spare his own Son' (Rom. 8:32, Gen. 22:12).

Jewish tradition shows with what tremendous force this story could act upon the soul, how near one could come, under its impression, to the sphere of Christ, to the Son's secret of death and resurrection.† 'When the sword came to Isaac's neck, his soul flew away from him. But when the voice of the Lord came from between the cherubim, "Lay not thy hand upon the boy," the soul came back into Isaac's body, Abraham unbound him and set him upon his feet. Then Isaac learned that there is a resurrection of the dead and that all the dead shall arise one day. In this hour he opened his mouth and said, "Praised be the Lord, who raises

★Words from the Creed of The Christian Community.

†Gorion, *Sagen der Juden* 2.292.

the dead".' Similarly, the Epistle to the Hebrews says of Abraham, 'He considered that God was able to raise men even from the dead; hence, figuratively speaking, he did receive him [Isaac] back' (Heb. 11:19).

Perhaps it has to do with this experience of death that in connection with Isaac a strange name of God is used: 'the God of Abraham and the Fear of Isaac', and Jacob swore 'by the Fear of his father Isaac.' (Gen. 31:42, 53). The Hebrew word *pachad* may well indicate the fear of death, the shuddering of Isaac as he approached the threshold of death.

Isaac's destiny was to wake the idea of death and resurrection. Out of death new life wells up.

To find life in death — is not that really the experience by a well? Turning from the bright sun of day, and bending over the edge of a well, one looks down into the night-black depths, but out of the darkness comes the silvery reflection of life. 'How strangely solemn and different from everyday life is one's mood on looking down into the depths, along the blackened, dripping sides of the well, down to the rippling mirror at the bottom. Suddenly one is no longer on the surface of life, but is gently touched by its depths. In the midst of the bright, sunny day one meets the eye of the dark and solemn night.'* Let us reflect how penetratingly the man of ancient times experienced such pictures, how symbolic the well must have been to the Orientals especially. Life upon the surface of earthly existence was condemned to thirst and burn in the searing, drying heat of the desert, unless the wells should reveal that other kingdom. There would be no life above in the light, in the white glow of midday without the beneficence of its depths, dark as a vault, cool as a grave,

> By death, eternal life was given to men
> And thou art death, and mak'st us whole again.†

*Kurt von Wistinghausen, *Die Christengemeinschaft* 1931:167.

†Novalis, *Hymns to the Night.*

118

This gives us the key to an intimate understanding of the fact that the 'Isaac' chapters are distinguished by their emphatic repetition of the motif of the well.

2 Beer-lahai-roi:
The Well of him who Lives and Sees

Isaac's wife Rebekah also is specially connected with the secret of the well. Abraham had sent his old servant Eliezer back to his home in Mesopotamia to seek the right wife for his son. One of the most poetical stories of the Old Testament tells how Eliezer rested with his camels by a well of water at the gate of the city and how in the cool of the evening the women and maidens came out of the city with their water-pots to draw water. Rebekah holds out her water pot in a friendly way to the old man and, unasked, gives water to the camels also. In this gesture Eliezer recognizes the bride whom providence has indicated. She follows him to Beer-sheba. One evening Isaac meets the returning caravan.

> Now Isaac had come from Beer-lahai-roi [the well of him that lives and sees] . . . And Isaac went out to meditate in the field in the evening. (Gen.24:62f).

The well of him who lives and sees — in this mysterious name the two gifts of the two trees of paradise seem to be united — life and knowledge. The man who sees God dies, but the man who rises out of this dying to a vision of God may unite his vision with life, which is now indeed a higher life. That this well was really a place of higher experience is shown also by the meeting which Hagar, the Egyptian, had there with the 'angel of the LORD' (Gen. 16:14).

Isaac led Rebekah into his mother Sarah's tent. (His mother had died three years before.) Thus 'Isaac was comforted after his mother's death.' Genesis presents Isaac as the 'son' who feels himself united in filial love to the mother. This is a small detail, but it is characteristic of the delicate manner of the description. Genesis speaks in this way only of Isaac.

Isaac lived for a long time by this well. Three and a half years after Isaac's marriage, Abraham died.

> *After the death of Abraham God blessed Isaac his son. And Isaac dwelt at Beer-lahai-roi (25:11).*

3 In the land of the Philistines

Unlike Abraham and Jacob, Isaac does not undertake great journeys. He never visits Babylonia or Egypt, but remains in the promised land. Only once during a famine he journeys to the land of the Philistines which is not far from Beer-sheba. Here enmity is roused against him, but he ultimately overcomes it, not by force, but by the quiet power of blessing which proceeds from him.

We see Isaac's intimate connection with the plant world. It is a fact that some people have 'green fingers' and plants flourish under their hands. In ancient times it was known that hands folded in prayer were hands blessed with the power over forces of life. It can be a blessing for the land when a farmer walks over it in reverence. We remember the words as Rebekah arrived, 'Isaac went out to meditate in the fields in the evening' (Gen.24:63).

Isaac is so strongly in league with the etheric forces of living things that the crops in his fields bear a hundredfold under his careful hands and eyes. 'The LORD blessed him' (26:12).

The Philistines became jealous, and

> *had stopped and filled with earth all the wells which his father's servants had dug in the days of Abraham his father (26:15).*

It is again characteristic of the style of these stories that we have heard nothing of those wells in the stories of Abraham, except the one in Beer-sheba. It is in connection with Isaac that we hear of wells. (Neither do we hear anything in

Genesis about Jacob's well which is mentioned in John's
Gospel).

> *And Isaac dug again the wells of water which had been dug in*
> *the days of Abraham his father; for the Philistines had stopped*
> *them after the death of Abraham; and he gave them the names*
> *which his father had given them. (26:18).*

Isaac brings to life again what was dead. He awakes to new
life the ruined wells of his father.

As he has shown himself to be filial to his mother, so now
Isaac shows himself to be filial in a special way to his father.
He not only opens up again his father's wells, he gives them
their names again. He 'gave them the names which his father
had given them.' This name-giving is a solemn ritual act.

Isaac also causes new wells to be dug. But he has no joy
because of the enmity of the Philistines.

'But Isaac's servants dug in the valley, and found there a
well of springing [living] water' (26:19). Yet the herdsman
of Gerar dispute with them saying, 'The water is ours.' And
the same thing happened by another well dug by Isaac's
servants. Therefore Isaac called the wells 'Esek' and
'Sitnah' — 'contention' and 'feud'. In perfect tranquillity he
caused a third well to be dug, and there was peace with the
brawlers. This well he called 'Rehoboth', 'broad places' or
'room'. The narrow, oppressive strife is over. Unrestricted
and untroubled now, his men can draw the water of this
well. 'Rehoboth' — 'broad places'.

4 Beer-sheba again

From there Isaac returned again to Beer-sheba. In the
night he received a divine revelation at this holy place. In
remembrance of it he built an altar at which he solemnly
called out God's name (26:25). Genesis tells of only one altar
which Isaac built — it is this altar at Beer-sheba. The special
connection of Isaac with this place of the cult is shown much
later. When Jacob, in very old age, goes down to Joseph in

Egypt, he breaks his journey at Beer-sheba, and there sacrifices 'to the God of his father Isaac', who blesses him 'in the visions of the night' (46:1,2). The God to whom Isaac builds his altar is El-Olam, who reveals his eternal nature in the 'dying' and 'rising again' of the cycle of time.

After the building of this altar Isaac 'pitched his tent there', and this pitching of a tent is followed immediately by the digging of a new well (26:25). The beginning of this digging and the crowning of the labour by the finding of water enclose significantly a scene of reconciliation and contentment. The king of the Philistines, who was before too jealous to bear to see Isaac in his land, whose subjects quarrelled with Isaac's servants about the well — this very king appears with two of his great men in Beer-sheba to change enmity into friendship. He has been deeply impressed by the quiet but great power of blessing which proceeds from the patriarch. To the latter's wondering question: 'Why have you come to me, seeing that you hate me and have sent me away from you?' they are constrained to reply: 'We see plainly that the LORD is with you . . . let us make a covenant with you . . . You are now the blessed of the LORD' (26:27,28f).

Isaac prepares a solemn feast for the three; next morning, at the hour of the early sacrifice, they swear a covenant and they depart from him in peace.

> That same day Isaac's servants came and told him about the well which they had dug, and said to him, 'We have found water.' (26:32).

Thus the whole story of the reconciliation, in which the power of Isaac's love overcame jealousy and enmity, is inserted into the account the digging of the well (26:25–32). This is not because the Bible wants to give a strict chronological account of it, but in order that the secret of the power of love, which brings peace at last, may be felt to be a 'secret of the well'.

In *Poetry and Truth* Goethe describes Abraham's 'calm and

122

greatness', and Isaac he characterizes by a subtle change of description: 'quietness and devotion'.

'Calm and greatness' like the nature of God himself. Calm and greatness comes to Abraham under the boughs of ancient, venerable oak trees.

'Quietness and devotion' is the mark of those who have looked into the cold well of death and found a higher life.

15. Jacob and the stones

It is characteristic of the third patriarch that stories about stones are told of him. In connection with Abraham and Isaac we hear nothing about stones. Jacob had his first great experience of God by the stone of Bethel.

1 The stone of Bethel

Jacob is fleeing from his brother Esau towards Haran and the East. 'And he came to a certain place, and stayed there that night' (Gen. 28:11). In the original text the words are more mysterious: 'he came to *the* place'. The essential quality of a 'place' is that it is a place of 'presence', that something is experienced as being present there. In this sense every being has its place somewhere or other in the cosmic being, whether in a higher or in a lower sphere. The primal picture of all these experiences of presence is the presence of the divine being; the place where one meets the divine being is *the* place.

That here in Genesis the word 'place' has a special meaning is shown by the repetition of the word three times in the first sentence of the story.

> *He came to a certain* place, *and stayed there that night, because the sun had set. Taking one of the stones of the* place, *he put it under his head and lay down in that* place *to sleep.*

This refers to an ancient group of stones, which had been set up in this 'place' like cromlechs. In the Holy Land as in other countries such stones were set up as memorials in prehistoric times. At this 'place' there still hovered something of the solemnity and magic of the ancient cosmic celebrations of the priests. Here without knowing it Jacob fell into a kind of 'temple sleep'. This sleep in the consecrated place was illuminated by the gentle, lucid light of clairvoyant dreams.

'Taking one of the stones of the place' (so there were several stones marking the place) Jacob took it for his pillow. The sacred text speaks of this stone in no trivial sense; it is not calling the attention of the reader to the hardness of this Spartan pillow so that the poverty of the homeless fugitive may be emphasized. If we contemplate the picture quietly for a little, we find that this juxtaposition of head and stone begins to speak. Head and stone. The 'cool' head, ruled by the mineral element of its bony structure, is it not related to the stone? Man's 'place of a skull' in which the intellectual thought has its abode, which understands only what is dead, which celebrates its triumphs only in the kingdom of dead matter, is leant against a stone. Stone upon stone! Is it not this head of clever Jacob in which the force of the 'clear head' has been awakened to an uncanny degree? This force which is so tragically strangled by lower egoism. And is not the awakening of the calculating, intellectual thinking of the head the sign that in Jacob heaven has been lost, and the last downward step into the earthly world has been taken?

It was not said of Abraham that he laid his head upon a stone, nor was it said of Isaac. But this picture 'looks like Jacob'. A more minute study of destiny may lead one to see that what happens to any man is always 'what is like him'. One has perceived the hidden configuration of a human life in grasping the fact that all the events are 'like' the person whose destiny it is to live it.

Those who, like Jacob, develop the forces of the head lose paradise. Jacob is far from the trees of Eden, which still cast their shade over Abraham. He is far from the waters of Eden which still spring up in Isaac's wells. Jacob, the most earthly of the patriarchs, lays his head upon a stone.

Here a special relationship is expressed. This is a sacred stone. On the one hand a stone can embody to an overwhelming extent the stark deadness of matter; in its hardness and coldness it marks the lowest point of the descent. But since it is this lowest point it may also become the foundation stone of a new ascent to the heavens. Just because it is the very lowest, it may point upwards to the very highest: it may support the ladder which reaches upward to the stars again. In this way, Jacob experienced the stone which he had laid for his head as the foundation stone of this whole vision of the ladder which reached upward to heaven. Observe the reverence with which he treats this stone when he awakes. But we anticipate, and will first let Jacob's experiences by night pass before us in detail.

The 'sun had set' when he placed the stone under his head. The day-consciousness disappears and the mysterious night-consciousness opens its starlike eyes.

> *And he dreamed, and behold, a ladder set up on the earth, and the top of it reached to heaven; and behold, the angels of God were ascending and descending on it. And behold, the LORD stood above it and said, 'I am the LORD . . .' (28:12f. Author's translation).*

The supersensory experience begins with the picture interwoven with light, with the *Imagination* which shines out before the eye of the soul (*behold* a ladder. . . . *behold* the angels of God), then it proceeds further to the perception of the divine words, revealed spiritual hearing, to *Inspiration* (the LORD said . . .)

Imagination, Inspiration. In the place of the third and highest stage, there is *Intuition*, the complete union of the knower with the known, so to speak the dread with which Jacob being awakened in the night becomes conscious of the *presence* of God.

Then Jacob awoke from his sleep and said, 'Surely the LORD is in this place; and I did not know it.' And he was afraid, and said, 'How awesome is this place! This is none other than the house of God, and this is the gate of heaven.' (28:16f).

This shuddering at the nearness of God belongs to the night. The following verse tells what happened next morning.

So Jacob rose early in the morning, and took the stone which he had put under his head and set it up for a pillar and poured oil on the top of it. He called the name of that place Bethel.

He set the stone up for a pillar — the stone which perhaps had been set up once before, a long time previously, when the old worship of heaven was at its zenith in this place, before it sank down into decay in the course of centuries, perhaps thousands of years. The upright stones, the 'menhirs' of prehistoric cults, were a great and unique proclamation of the forces which raise bodies upright. The weight of earthly things, the dull heavy resistance of matter, is overcome by this force which morning by morning makes a man stand upright, raises him from the 'position of a corpse,' as Albert Steffen says. The mystery of 'setting up,' which so intimately touches mankind, was the Gospel proclaimed with simplicity and power by this upright stone.

In the morning a man stands up from sleep. In the morning Christ rose again from the grave. Standing upright is a mystery of the early morning. In the sacred morning hour, after the night of divine illumination, Jacob set up the stone.

In order to consecrate it he 'poured oil on the top of it.' In the original this is 'on the *head*' of the stone. Here again we have the motif: stone, head. The golden oil is specially the bearer of consecration. 'Christ' means 'anointed'. The 'head' of this stone which has been lifted up is 'anointed with oil', the hard is blessed with the soft, the earthly is made golden with light.

To the spectator this occurrence seems like a prophetic hieroglyph. Because such a thing is told of Jacob who had descended most deeply into earthly things we can surmise that the the lowest and most earthly thing may, just because it is so, become the foundation, the base and the support of a new ascent. He who has reached the bottom of the valley is in a sense nearer the heights than he who has not yet descended so low but is still coming down the slope. In this earth world, which is very far from paradise, the clear awakened head, the activity of the intellect which one acquires 'at the stone', is intended to find its way back again to the divine. What Jacob did in subconscious prophecy when he set up this hieroglyph may perhaps be expressed more abstractly thus: It is the spiritualizing of intellectual thought, the hallowing of the strong forces of earth, which a man can acquire in the region of the dead material world. It is a prophecy of the time of the Holy Spirit, when the way shall have been found again from the stone to the stars.

In the trinity of the patriarchs, Jacob is the representative of, or to put it more modestly, he stands for the Holy Spirit. This may at first seem strange. But, if we may speak so humanly, it was comparatively easy for Providence to fill the roles of 'father' and 'son', to find in Abraham and Isaac worthy representatives of these sublime divine principles. But on the other hand it was much more difficult to find a worthy representative for the third. That one cannot yet be found who fits this role completely shows that this third divine principle is by nature connected with the *future*. Only through Christ will the Holy Spirit be able to enter into man. It is no chance that in the third patriarch we feel especially the discrepancy between the representative and what he represents.

It is noticeable that the word 'head' is a key-word in the whole narrative. Jacob placed the stone 'under his head' (28:11); the 'head' of the ladder (literal translation) reached to heaven (28:12); he took the stone which he had put under his 'head', and he poured oil on the 'head' of it (literal translation, 28:18). Emil Bock reminds us of the Babylonian expression 'the elevation of the head'.★

With the anointing of the stone is connected the *giving of the name*. In solemn ceremony Jacob calls out the name of the place: 'Bethel', 'the house of God'.

The end of the sacred morning service is the vow which Jacob vowed. If what has been promised in the vision by night should be fulfilled, if Jacob should be guarded on his way and should return home in peace, if he shall have food and raiment, then here he will build a house of God and give him tithe.

Abraham gave tithe to Melchizedek. The tithe was given in order that consecrated and sacred persons should be able to have an existence upon earth. Jacob was to give to the 'God of Bethel' his tithe.

In this is mirrored a great truth. After man has got a firm footing upon earth by the unfolding of his egotistic power, after he has built for himself an earthly house, then there must be awakened in him devotion to the divine. When earthly man turns in sacrifice to the Godhead, then the Godhead can find through man an entrance into the 'earthly world', which before was possessed only by egoism. Earthly man when he turns to sacrifice helps to build 'Bethel', the house of God upon earth.

In distinction from the mood of Buddha who feels that earth must be renounced, that the work of the 'housebuilder' must be destroyed, the conception of the 'house of God' contained in the Bible, is very important. It finds its fulfilment in the Christmas mystery of the *Incarnation* of the divine.

So we find a deep meaning in the fact that the sacred place of the most earthly of the patriarchs is Bethel, the house of God. The descent to Jacob's level was also necessary to prepare for the descent of God into an earthly body.

★*Genesis*, p. 156

2 The stone on the well

Immediately after the story of Bethel we have the story of
the well in the east.

> Then Jacob went on his journey, and came to the land of the
> people of the east. As he looked, he saw a well in the field . .
> The stone on the well's mouth was large (29:1,2).

After the holy night in Bethel, Jacob continues his way to
the place from which Abraham had once come. 'In the east
lies the garden of Eden. The way to the east, is the way to
the rejuvenating, life-giving forces.

At the well he meets Rachel. Like Rebekah before this,
and Zipporah, the bride of Moses afterwards, Rachel appears
first beside the well, in union with its ethereal life-forces.
But this story of a well (the only one told of Jacob) contains
also the characteristic of the experiences of Jacob: upon the
well lies *a great stone*. It is Jacob's destiny to be obliged
always to struggle against obstacles. Thus he must overcome
obstacles in winning Rachel also. For her he must serve
twice seven years. This picture also is 'like him'. By *his own
strength* he must *roll the stone from the well*.

The herdsmen want to wait until they have all assembled.
Only by a common effort, out of the power of their
collective force, can they open up the well.

> Now when Jacob saw Rachel . . . Jacob went up and rolled
> the stone from the well's mouth . . .

The man whose strength is increased by the resistance of
the stone, so that he overcomes its weight, can find access
to the water of life which flows from the well towards the
morning, and he wins the bride.

3 The stone of Gilead

During the twenty years there in the east Jacob became rich.
After that he returns home, now no longer a poor fugitive,
but a patriarch, with Rachel and Leah and the children, a

train of servants, and large flocks and herds. Laban persues him, hunts the wanderer who is returning home; but in a vision he is warned not to act against Jacob in an unfriendly manner. He makes a covenant with him upon the mount of Gilead, where he has caught up with him. Again it is characteristic of Jacob that he sets up a *pillar of stone* as testimony to the compact. The like is never told of Abraham or of Isaac.

> *So Jacob took a stone, and set it up for a pillar* [maçebhah]. *And Jacob said to his kinsmen, 'Gather stones,' and they took stones, and made a heap; and they ate there by the heap (31:45f).*

Just as Abraham was priest under the sacred tree, so Jacob celebrated the cult of the stone. He set up the stone and surrounded it by a circle of stones. It is easy to see that this stone had a sacramental significance. There the covenant was sworn by Jacob and Laban. It is also clear that the eating is not merely a meal, but a sacramental repast. Then

> *Jacob offered a sacrifice on the mountain and called his kinsmen to eat bread; and they ate bread and tarried all night on the mountain (31:54).*

At the stone circle upon the height of the sacred mountain, the cult of sacrifice was celebrated, and in connection with this the sacramental meal of peace was held. That they also remained there *all night* denotes again an experience of a 'temple sleep'. This time, however, we are not told of any clairvoyant dreams at the consecrated spot. Immediately afterwards we are told of a meeting with angels.

> *Jacob went on his way and the angels of God met him; and when Jacob saw them, he said, 'This is God's army!' So he called the name of the place Manahaim. (32:2f).*

The immediate succession of the experiences of Gilead and Manahaim is scarcely fortuitous. It is certain that the sacramental act performed beside the sacred stone on the mountain, the sacrifice and meal of the cult, and the sleep under the stars, had all combined to lay open Jacob's soul to a vision of the angels, like that which he had before at Bethel. This time it was not a dream, but as he was on his way it came into his clear day consciousness, the consciousness of the man who has just set up a sacred stone.

4 The return to Bethel

After the vision of the angels at Mahanaim Jacob meets the angel at the Jabbok ford and wrestles until dawn to extract a blessing. He calls this place 'Peniel', 'the face of God'.

Following the meeting with Esau Jacob settles at Shechem. He buys some land and builds an altar there which he calls 'El-Elohe-Israel', 'the God who is God of Israel'. Israel is the name he is given by the angel at Peniel, 'he who strives with God'. The changing of his name shows, as with Abraham, an inner development. He has become another, or one could say, more 'like himself'. Now as an individual he carries the name of the whole people who will be his descendants.

We see in the third patriarch again a connection with the Holy Spirit. At Whitsun the Holy Spirit founds a new community, the Church. Jacob here becomes the founder of the people Israel, who are made up of twelve tribes, as the Church is founded on the twelve Apostles.

Later Jacob is told by God to go to Bethel. What he had experienced as he set out upon his journey on that holy night remained for him *the* experience of his life. The stone of Bethel had become for him the foundation stone of his religious consciousness. Just as the grove of Mamre may be called Abraham's place, and the city of the well, Beer-sheba, Isaac's place, so Bethel may be called the place of Jacob.

Even into a foreign land he had been accompanied by the memory of it. While he is still dwelling with Laban in the east, he speaks to Rachel and Leah of a dream in which the voice of God says: 'I am the God of Bethel, where you anointed a pillar' (31:13). So we can understand why after

his stay in Shechem he again seeks a place which is so
important to him. A special call from God points the way.

> God said to Jacob, 'Arise, go up to Bethel, and dwell there;
> and make there an altar to the God who appeared to you when
> you fled from your brother Esau.' (35:1).

This journey to Bethel, which is a kind of pilgrimage, is
preceded by an act of ceremonial purification. The 'foreign
gods' and ear-rings (a kind of amulet) which his servants had,
were removed and buried under the old oak by Shechem.

In Bethel, Jacob now builds an altar, which is in a special
sense *his* altar. This is the last of the seven altars built by the
patriarchs of which we are told in Genesis. Four of these
were erected by Abraham: at the oak of Shechem (12:7),
upon a mountain near Bethel (12:8), in the grove of Mamre
(13:18), upon Mount Moriah (22:9). Isaac's altar stood at
Beer-sheba (26:25), Jacob built an altar in Shechem (33:20),
and now, completing the number, he builds the seventh in
Bethel (35:7): 'and there he built an altar, and called the place
El-bethel; because there God had revealed himself to him
when he fled from his brother'.

This cult of sacrifice at the altar of Bethel was the response
to the new revelations of God.

> God appeared to Jacob again, when he came from Paddan-
> aram [Mesopotamia], and blessed him. And God said to him,
> 'Your name is Jacob; no longer shall your name be called Jacob,
> but Israel shall be your name.'. . . Then God went up
> from him in the place where he had spoken with him.
> (35:9,13).

The objection has been raised that we have already been
told of this change of the name of Jacob into 'Israel' in the
story of the wrestling with the angel by night at Peniel, at
the ford of the river Jabbok (32:28); and it has been said that
here we have another 'reading', according to which the
change of name took place not at Peniel, but at Bethel. But
we must understand this passage in the sense that the
experience by night — the struggle with the angel — has an

133

inward connection with the experience at Bethel, which is the most important among all Jacob's experiences. Many and varied spiritual experiences may exist side by side in the soul; it needs time to let them grow together into an organic whole. Until now the mysterious experience of that struggle by night was as it were isolated in Jacob's memory; it had not been integrated in his soul with the earlier experience of Bethel. Now, when Jacob is back in Bethel, there occurs this unifying of his inward revelations: the two great meetings with God. The gift of the name Israel, God's warrior, received for the first time at dawn at Peniel was strengthened and confirmed at his own place, Bethel.

Similarly it may be a mistake of modern biblical interpretation to speak of a 'doublet' when it finds a repetition of the sacred acts: setting up a stone and anointing it. It is true that the same thing occurs again which had previously occurred on the morning after the night when Jacob dreamed of the ladder which reached up to heaven.

> *And Jacob set up a pillar in the place where he had spoken with him, a pillar of stone; and he poured a drink offering on it, and he poured oil on it. So Jacob called the name of the place where God had spoken with him, Bethel. (35:14f).*

This doing of the same thing again is in reality the recurrence of the experience that lay three times seven years behind him. Jacob performs this act of repetition as a concrete 'in memoriam' of the original act. And by doing so he brings the act back again out of the past into the present. So he has really returned to Bethel. One might almost say he has returned home.

The fact that the place is three times solemnly named 'Beth-El', as in a solemn baptism, gives the name a quite special importance (28:19; 35:7; 35:15).

To the last hours of Jacob's life this experience echoed in his soul. The dying patriarch calls his twelve sons to his death-bed and prophesies to them. As he blesses Joseph he calls the Godhead by a unique name, he calls it the 'stone of

Israel' (49:24 literal translation). God is for him connected with the stone, the 'foundation stone'.

5 *The stone on Rachel's grave*

The first experience at Bethel was followed by the meeting with Rachel at the well. The second story in Bethel was followed by Rachel's death. The relation of Jacob to Rachel, among all the relations between man and wife in the age of the patriarchs, is the most personal and individual. Rachel was not brought to him by the servant as Rebekah was brought to Isaac. He had chosen her personally, had worked for her and won her. She was taken from him by an early death. She died when Benjamin was born.

> . . . and Jacob set up a pillar upon her grave; it is the pillar of Rachel's tomb, which is there to this day. (35:20).

When he met Rachel at the well towards morning, he rolled the stone from the well. Now that gracious gift, which then had entered his life, disappears from it again. Jacob's life is a prophecy; it is not yet fulfilment. For only a short space of his long life could he be united with Rachel, the mystical 'bride' who came from the well in the east. The most earthly of the patriarchs, he who descended most deeply into 'incarnation', must taste the bitterest tragedy of earth. The last stone he sets up is a gravestone. It is as if the well were covered again by the stone.

Upon Rachel's grave stands the stone — fit expression of the tragedy of human destiny, in its implacable hardness and frigid silence. But the stone is not only a heavy, dead mass; it is set up as a memorial pillar. It is an anticipation; it is a beginning of the conquest of the 'stone' by the forces which set things upright.

In this story of Rachel's death we have a special prophecy: Rachel died upon the way 'to Ephrath (that is, Bethlehem)' (35:19). How marvellously the lines of destiny are inter-twined! Bethlehem: There the boy Jesus will be born one day, and through him God will enter this earthly world. There the prophecy of Bethel, the 'House of God', will be fulfilled. And Mary will take the place of Rachel, in whom the 'eternal feminine', the morning forces of the tree of life, enter Jacob's life for a time.

From Sabbath to Sunday

16. Sunday: A Christian fact

1 Sunday in danger

If our solar year had only 364 days it could be divided exactly by seven, which is the number of days in a week. In that case the dates of every year would have the same day. For example Christmas Day would always fall on the same weekday. As it is, the year has an extra day with the result that each year the days of the week move on from the date. If your birthday is on Monday this year, next year it will be on Tuesday or in the case of a leap-year on Wednesday.

This rotation of the days of the week in the course of the years is anathema to certain would-be calendar reformers who would like to make the year's cycle correspond once and for all with the week's cycle. The extra (365th) day would be 'neutralized'. As the year cannot be shortened by a day, these so-called reformers would like to remove the surplus day from the week, giving it a non-weekday name. They would wait until a year comes when December 30 is on a Saturday. They would then make January 1 a Sunday for all time, and declare December 31 an empty day with no weekday name and instead call it a 'world-holiday'. In a leap-year they suggest doing the same at the end of June.

For thousands of years Sunday has followed Saturday. This rhythm of our lives would be broken. It is difficult to understand why Christendom has not risen to a man to defend itself against this proposition which touches the very nerve of Christian religious practice. Apparently there is no

137

real sense of what such a break in the rhythm would mean. Hitherto the Christian Sunday has been week after week the exact and uninterrupted 'octave' of the Easter-Resurrection-Day, but now it would no longer be a 'true' Sunday. Is that so very important? One cannot answer this question until one understands how the seven-day week and the Christian celebration of Sunday have come about.

2 The Chaldean planetary week

The names of the weekdays are familiar and well known from olden times. Few people think anything of it. But let us just ask ourselves, what sort of names are they? With Sunday and Monday the connection to Sun and Moon is immediately apparent. Tuesday is harder to recognize. It bears within it the name of the Germanic god of war Tiw. In Wednesday the god Wodan (Odin) can be found, in Thursday we find the god Thor, in Friday the goddess Freya. Saturday, however, originates from the Roman god Saturnus, the Greek Kronos. In spite of the Germanic names of the gods the seven-day week is in all probability not an indigenous Germanic institution, but was taken over from the Romans. Through the western tribes of the Franks and Alemanni it was brought further east and north, while the old gods were worshipped before Christianity was paramount.

The week, then, was a pre-Christian planet-god week which spread by way of the Rhine and the Danube. Seven ancient pagan gods gave their names to the days of the week: Sun-god, Moon-goddess, Mars, Mercury, Jupiter, Venus and Saturn. In Greek: Helios, Selene, Ares, Hermes, Zeus, Aphrodite and Kronos. The Germanic peoples applied the names of their own corresponding gods, thus Tiw for warlike Mars; Thor and further south Donar for Jupiter. Donar is still to be found in the German *Donnerstag*. In the Romance languages the Latin names survive: the French *jeudi* comes from *Jovis dies*, *vendredi* from *Veneris dies*, *mercredi* from Mercury, the messenger god.

The worship of these seven gods of the days seems to have flourished particularly in the Romano-Germanic border areas during the third Christian century. A considerable amount of monumental stones representing the seven has been found east and west of the Rhine.

But the origin of the week is not even to be found with the Romans. The ancient Romans themselves had a kind of eight-day week whereby the farmers after seven working days brought their produce to the market on the eighth. The seven-day week first found its way into the Roman Empire shortly before the beginning of the Christian era, coming by way of Egypt, though Egypt was not its cradle. The planetary week originated in the eastern centre of culture which in the ancient world had the reputation of possessing the deepest knowledge and wisdom of the stars: Chaldea. It began with Saturday in the sign of Ninib which corresponded to Saturn. Then followed Shamash: Sun; Sin: Moon; Nergal: Mars; Nebo: Mercury; Marduk: Jupiter; Ishtar: Venus. Romans and Greeks and later the Teutons applied their own corresponding names.

Was this Chaldean 'star-wisdom' perhaps rather primitive? Modern people are inclined to remark that Sun and Moon are not 'proper' planets, and that Uranus, Neptune and Pluto are missing, not to mention the planetoids. We should however arrive at a more just appreciation of these ancient cultures if we would accept the idea that the men of those days did not think and pursue their research in a modern, scientific way, but that they used quite different faculties of perception which have since been lost; for should we not also allow that man's consciousness itself has undergone a variety of transformations and developments? Of course the seven planets of the Chaldeans do not coincide with what we today regard as the planetary system. What is important here is to note that the ancient septuary of the planets was a result of direct visual observation. The way in which phenomena present themselves to the senses is important, for the senses are in fact designed in accordance with the reality of the world. The seven celestial luminaries present themselves to the eye as planets which move against the background of the fixed stars. Yet to the deeper contemplation of the ancients their individual 'qualities' were revealed.

It is not surprising that a great deal of superstition has attached itself to the number seven. But we should not throw out the baby with the bath-water. In connection with the number seven several observations from different fields of existence could be adduced, and these must give us food for thought. In fact its function is to bring things into order in many different ways.

The order of the seven 'planets', or spirits of the stars, in the days of the week is remarkable, as the spatial arrangement is not just projected into time; for the spatial ordering would make Jupiter and Mars follow Saturn in order of distance, and then the other three, Venus, Mercury and the Moon, whose periods of revolution are shorter than the sun's year, would also be together. But in fact near and far planets follow each other alternately. The order goes from Saturn via the Sun to the near Moon, then back out to Mars and in again to fast-moving Mercury; from Mercury to distant, slow Jupiter, and in again to Venus, and from this slowest of the inner planets out again to the slowest of the outer planets, Saturn, whose period of revolution requires as many years as the Moon's requires days. It is like an in and out-breathing between near and far.

This ordering of the week spread through the Roman Empire in the first century BC. In the Roman literature of that time the Saturn-Day appears. The poet Tibullus (54–19 BC) mentions the observance of the hallowed Saturn-Day as a possible obstacle to leaving his home place (*Saturni sacram me tenuisse diem*). In the first two Christian centuries the planetary week completely established itself. The famous magician Apollonius of Tyana (first century) placed a different ring on his finger for each of the seven days. With the excavations in Pompeii and Herculaneum inscriptions and pictures have been brought to light which name and represent the seven day-gods, and which must have been created before AD 79, the year of the eruption of Vesuvius. Dio Cassius writes about AD 210–220 that 'the arrangement of the days according to the seven so-called planets has been accepted by all peoples — though I do not believe since very long. It is customary with all peoples and even with the Romans.' (37.18). That was during the reign of Septimus Severus who thought highly of the Chaldean astrology and who built a temple to the seven day-gods on the Palatine.

3 The Jewish week

It is a remarkable fact that during these same centuries the seven-day week was spreading in another form, namely through Judaism. There were Jewish congregations everywhere in the Roman Empire. It was just at that time that the Diaspora Jews who had been scattered abroad were involved in successful missionary work. Many gentile seekers, no longer content with the decadent pagan cults, were attracted by the strict monotheism and by the ethical nature of the Ten Commandments, and approached Judaism as sympathizers or as proselytes. The sabbath as a day of rest after every six working days was adopted in many circles.

Philo of Alexandria, a Jewish mystic and philosopher of the Logos, who lived at the time of Jesus Christ (20 BC to AD 54) was able to write: 'The sabbath is held in honour by the foremost Hellenes and Barbarians' (De Opif. M. 43). And the Jewish historian Josephus (AD 37–?100) expressed with pride: 'Also much enthusiasm for our religion is to be found among the masses, and there is no nation, no Greek or Barbarian city, where our custom of resting from work on the seventh day has not gained entrance.' (*C.Ap.* 2.89). In his biography of Tiberius (Ch.32) Suetonius tells of a grammarian Diogenes, who at that time lived on Rhodes, that he was in the habit of holding his disputations 'only on the sabbath', and still in pre-Christian times we encounter the sabbath in the writings of the poet Horace (63–8 BC). In his satires (1.9,60–74) he mentions an amusing episode which however can also be regarded as symptomatic. Horace wishes to free himself from an importunate companion who has joined him in the street. He hopes to be relieved by his friend Fuscus Aristius who happens to cross his path at just the right moment. 'Could not the two of us discuss an important matter privately?' But his friend lets him down sharply. 'Another time!' This friend is a Roman like Horace, but he says: 'Not today. Today is the sabbath.' Horace replies that *he* does not feel himself constrained on religious grounds, whereupon his friend retorts: 'But *I* do! I need something to support me — one of many.'

The sabbath has left further traces with Ovid (43 BC–AD 17), Martial (AD 58–100) and Juvenal (AD 47–130). The latter sees in the celebration of the sabbath only a reluctance to work and condemns the Romans for adopting such a custom. 'But the father is to blame for always being lazy on the seventh day and for not touching the least thing of his business.' (*Sat.* 14.105). The biting vituperation of a man like Seneca (AD 4–65) proves how far the observance of the sabbath had already penetrated Roman circles. He maintains that the Jews lose a seventh part of their lives through idleness: 'In the meantime the custom of this wretched people has become so prevalent as to be adopted in all countries, and this means that the vanquished are imposing their laws upon the victors.' (quoted from St Augustine *De Civ. Dei* 6.11). He wrote: 'Let us put a stop to this lighting of the sabbath lamps by all kinds of people.' These protests were fruitless.

In contrast with the Chaldean the Jewish week does not begin with Saturday but with Sunday leading up to the sabbath as the crowning of the week. It was known that the Jewish sabbath coincided with the Saturn-Day of the Chaldean week (Dion Cassius 37.17) but for the rest the Jewish week had quite a different character.

Providence had given the Jews the task of developing a wakeful consciousness of the 'I'. This consciousness was to be the preparation for the Christ, for the 'I am' spoken in clear, calm self-awareness. In Judaism there arose an intellectual thinking capable of protecting the developing free personality from the incursions and domination of obsure dreamlike soul states. Abraham, the initiator of this new spirituality, by his wandering forth, freed himself from the womb of the Babylonian-Chaldean culture which had centres of moon and star-worship in Ur and Haran (Gen. 11:28, 31).

The star-wisdom of the Chaldeans, founded upon ancient powers, and fallen into decadence, could not lead into the future. Progress necessitated the transition to a consciousness of the 'I' which although primarily abstract was nevertheless firm in itself and pure fundamentally.

We cannot be surprised then that the Jewish week, though looking back to Chaldea in its aspect of a seven-day rhythm, bears no more trace of the planetary character of the individual days. In the Jewish week Sunday is not the day of the Sun, but the 'first day after the sabbath'. Monday is then 'the second', and so on.

The numbering of the days which appears to us so dry and calculating had still in those days a last echo of 'quality', because for the ancient world the numbers were not so external and colourless as they are today. In the story of Creation in Genesis the seven days of creation are numbered with a certain solemnity. The Jewish week stood in the afterglow of this exalted archetypal week, but we cannot deny that in comparison with the powerfully pictorial day-gods the Jewish week has become abstract.

Apart from the Creation itself the soul's rhythmic experience of the seven days appears early in the Old Testament. One week before the beginning of the Flood Noah receives the last warning from God (Gen. 7:4–10). Towards the end of the Flood the seven days again play a part with the sending out of the dove (Gen. 8:8–12). At Jacob's wedding the seven days are kept (Gen. 29:27f), as later with Samson (Judg. 14:12–17). We find them also in the observances of a death. Joseph mourned for his father for seven days (Gen. 50:10). Several centuries later seven days' lamentation were made for King Saul (1 Sam. 31:13).

In the Law of Moses the sabbath is not introduced but re-emphasized: 'Remember the sabbath day, to keep it holy' (Exod. 20:8). At the time of the Passover unleavened bread is eaten for seven days (Lev. 23:6). For seven days the Feast of the Tabernacles is celebrated (Lev. 23:34). Seven days were needed for the consecration of Solomon's Temple (1 Kings 8:65). A culmination of the experiencing of the week came every year between the Passover and the Jewish Pentecost. The latter pertained to the ingathering of the harvest and also to the celebration of the Ten Commandments which were given to Moses on Mount Sinai seven weeks before the exodus from Egypt. This Old Testament Pentecost was called 'Shebuoth' meaning the 'seven-ness', the 'weeks'. Admittedly that does not prove that the seven day week has rolled on without interruption from earliest times. The scanty sources do not allow that to be established with certainty. But what does stand assured is the fact that at least since the exile in Babylon, that is since the sixth century BC, the continuation of the seven day week has not suffered any interruption. Thus the sabbath today is irrefutably the exact octave of the sabbath of at least two and a half thousand years ago. With its innate tenacity Jewry has preserved its sabbath through all kinds of calendar situations obtaining among its host nations right up to the present day. With that the 'genuineness' of our present-day Christian Sunday as the repetition of the Day of Resurrection is guaranteed.

4 The Christian Sunday

From the background of divine worlds Christianity entered earth history through the event upon Golgotha. The institution of the seven-day week can be regarded in all earnestness as an act of Providence relating to the appearance of the divinity upon earth, for the 'Incarnation of the Word' does not merely mean that the invisible revealed itself in an earthly body, visible in space to the eye of man, but also that it entered the course of time. From the supra-temporal it entered the sequence of the temporal and thus became a historical fact. Thus the eternal entered the course of the 'three years' from the Baptism in Jordan. Thus it entered the format of the seven day week when it enacted the central deed of Death and Resurrection. The Holy Week, as a 'form' in time, receives the great mystery into itself, whereby Palm Sunday with its rejoicing is like a pre-octave to the Sunday of Resurrection, which in its turn initiates the seven weeks that lead to Whitsun.

The day which hitherto in Judaism only bore the name of the 'first after the sabbath' now received a decisive accentuation. Thenceforth for Christian sentiment it is inseparable from the Resurrection.

The thinking observer of history must constantly ask the question, how was it possible for the early Christian communities who were so deeply rooted in the Old Testament to make the transition from the celebration of the sabbath to that of Sunday. We hear of no decree by the apostles whereby the commandment given upon Sinai to keep the sabbath holy is to be applied to another day. The sabbath was kept at first, but it gradually lost its importance as the new Christian day prevailed as a matter of course. At the so-called Council of the Apostles (in the middle of the century) it was laid down what was the minimum obligation to the laws of the Old Testament to be demanded of the heathens adopting Christianity. They are enjoined to abstain from the flesh of animals that have not been slaughtered, but of an observance of the sabbath we hear nothing (Acts 15:20).

Only by taking into account the all-powerful impress of Easter can we understand how 'the first day' gradually superseded the sabbath in importance. God did not proclaim a new law for Sunday through a new Moses, but he let the Christ rise from the dead — on Sunday. A deed spoke. From that day, Sunday was 'the day which the Lord had made'. Sunday as a recurring octave made itself felt in religious experience with compelling power. The genius of the Russian language gives a wonderful expression to this experience by calling Sunday *Voskresenye*, 'Resurrection'.

John's Gospel tells us of the first octave experience. The Risen One reveals himself to doubting Thomas 'eight days later', (20:26) and indeed so realistically that Thomas has to confess: 'my Lord and my God'. And just as after the week of weeks, the seven times seven days after the Passover the Jews celebrated Pentecost, so now the fiftieth day (*Pentēcostē* in Greek means the fiftieth), the seventh octave of the Easter event, becomes the Christian Pentecost, Whitsun. Thus Sunday is also anchored in Christendom by the Festival of the Holy Spirit.

5 The Lord's Day

In the New Testament at first the Jewish nomenclature of The 'first day after the sabbath' is retained. We find this 'first day' in the Easter chapters of all four evangelists (Matt.28:1, Mark 16:2, Luke 24:1, John 20:1,19), and Paul also uses this form. In the First Letter to the Corinthians 'the first day of every week' (16:2) is implied as the usual day for the assembly of the Christian congregations. That would be about the year 54. The Acts of the Apostles tells how the congregation of Troas were gathered together with Paul by night on the first day after the sabbath, which of course ended at six o'clock on Saturday evening; and the rite of the 'breaking of bread' was celebrated early on Sunday morning before the first rays of the rising sun (20:7–11).

At the end of the New Testament however, in the Revelation to John, a new name with greater content is introduced. John, now an old man on Patmos, beholds the all-powerful sun-filled appearance of the Risen One on the 'Lord's Day' (1:10).

The new name now becomes general. About AD 107 Bishop Ignatius of Antioch, the martyr, warns the Church of Magnesia (Ch.9) against back-sliding into the sabbath cult which he calls *sabbatizein*, 'to sabbathize'. He exhorts them rather to live *kata kyriakēn*, according to the Lord's Day, 'on which our life has arisen'. Ignatius shows that he is filled with the knowledge that the Lord's Day is something quite new and quite distinct from the sabbath. It is not the 'Christian sabbath'; it has in fact nothing to do with the sabbath; it is quite different altogether.

The word 'Kyrios' played a part in the cult of Caesar. Domitian called himself officially 'Lord and God'. However, there is abundant material showing that the word 'Kyrios' was also used particularly for the Sun God.*

6 The day of the sun

It is in harmony with the foregoing that a third name should appear. In AD 150 the martyr and philosopher Justin presented a defence, an *apologia*, to the Roman Emperor which was addressed at the same time to the educated Greco-

*F. J. Dölger, *Sol Salutis*.

Roman world. For the first time — among the documents we know to date — the expression 'day of the sun' is used (*Ap.* 1.67). In broad outline Justin describes the course of a Christian service as celebrated 'on the day of the sun'. He adds: 'For that is the first day on which God transformed the darkness and the original matter (*hulē*) and created a cosmos.' According to Justin's world-view a kind of original substance, wrapped in darkness, already existed at the time when the Creation, described in Genesis, began and the Word resounded: 'Let there be light'. Justin builds a wonderful bridge from this 'Let there be light' to the Easter event: 'On the selfsame first day our Saviour Jesus Christ rose from the dead. On the day before the Kronos-Saturn Day they crucified him, and after the Kronos Day, on the day which is the day of the Sun, he appeared to his apostles.'

It should not be forgotten that the Apologia is not directed to those within Christian circles, but is intended to be understood by 'outsiders'. Nevertheless such a pronounced Christian as Justin the Martyr must have considered it permissable to use the cosmic names Saturn-day and Sun-day. His allusion to 'Let there be light' stands in harmony with the 'day of the sun'.

Early Christendom did not by any means exclude the content of other 'pagan' non-biblical world-views, for Christianity was not felt to be just the continuation and sublimation of the Old Testament, but the rightful heir to all the true spiritual possessions of humanity. That is implicit in the words of Paul: 'For all things are yours' (1Cor.3:21). A Christianity which cherishes these words of Paul: 'You are Christ's' (1Cor.3:23) can regard as justified that 'the glory of the nations'* should be included in the heavenly Jerusalem as this Christianity gazes forth with the vision of the revelation of John (Rev.21:24–26).

A link with the sun-character of the Resurrection Day is

---

*The 'nations' in the Bible refers to the gentiles, the heathens.

already inherent in the Gospels. Mark says of the Easter morn: 'And very early on the first day of the week . . . when the sun had risen' (16:2). The sun-nature of the being who could say: 'I am the light of the world' (John 9:5) appears in important places in the New Testament. At the Transfiguration upon the mount his countenance shone 'like the sun' (Matt. 17:2). He appears to Paul before Damascus at the midday hour as a light 'brighter than the sun' (Acts 26:13). John on Patmos sees his countenance 'like the sun shining in full strength' (Rev. 1:16). For early Christendom the appellation of the Lord's Day as The 'day of the sun' was directly illuminating.

St Jerome (340–420) writes: 'When the day which the Lord has made, that is the Day of Resurrection, is called the day of the sun by the heathen, we may gladly accept this designation; for today [Easter Sunday] the Light of the World, the Sun of Righteousness has arisen' (*Comm. Ps.* 118). Likewise Maximus of Turin (around 460) writes: 'The Day of Resurrection is for us so to be honoured, because on this day the Saviour after overcoming the darkness in the underworld, shone forth like the rising sun in the light of the Resurrection. Therefore this day is called the "day of the sun" by the people of the world (*homines saeculi*) because Christ, the Rising Sun of Righteousness illuminates it with his light.' (*Hom.* 61). The expression 'Sun of Righteousness', comes from the Old Testament. Significantly it is to be found at the end of the last book of the prophets, Malachi (4:2). Christian preachers and writers repeatedly refer to this passage.

Noteworthy is what Tertullian in two of his writings has to say (*Ad nat.* 1.13, and *Apol. adv. gent.* 16). 'Others [of our antagonists] believe with more humanity and probability that the Sun is our God. When we are accounted to be Persians . . . I believe that that comes from our well-known custom of praying towards the east.' He reminds the heathens: 'It is you who have taken the sun into your calendar of seven days.' He complains that they improperly observe the Day of Saturn through Jewish influence. On March 7, 321 the Emperor Constantine promulgated a memorable law, raising the 'worshipful Day of the Sun' to a legally protected holy day. Coming as he did from an ancient sun-cult he thought to satisfy therewith both Christian and heathen sun-worshippers.

7 Shades of confusion

We can observe how the Christianity of the first centuries had largely adopted the planetary week, and this not only with regard to the sun's day. We remember how Justin quite freely speaks of Holy Saturday as the day of Kronos-Saturn. Likewise Clement of Alexandria calls Wednesday and Friday the day of Hermēs-Mercury and the day of Aphrodite-Venus (*Strom.* 75.2). Christian inscriptions relating to the time between 269 and 473 have been discovered, and these prove that even in Christian circles the planetary names were used here and there.

This obviously caused reservations. The established Church, with its strong Old Testament colouring, shied away from this cosmic connection, even retreating from the 'Sun-Day'. The strictly orthodox Emperor Theodosius recommended the return to the earlier usage when 'our forefathers rightly called the "day of the sun" the "Lord's Day".' In the times following, the 'day of the sun' disappeared from official approval. The Romance languages have adapted themselves to this. They have dropped the 'day of the sun' and have returned to the 'Day of the Lord'. The derivation from *dies dominica* is clearly recognizable in the French *dimanche*, Italian *domenica* and Spanish *domingo*. It may be because of a stronger feeling for the natural and cosmic that the northern peoples in contrast to the usage of the Latin Church, have held fast to the sun. German *Sonntag*, English *Sunday*, Dutch *zondag*, Norwegian *søndag*.

We can feel an unmistakable unease in St Augustine when he speaks of the planetary week. He asserts rather vexatiously: 'The first day after the sabbath is the Lord's Day. The second day after the sabbath is the "Second Day" [*secunda feria*], laymen [*saeculares*] call it the "Day of the Moon". They call the third, Day of Mars. The fourth is called Mercury's Day by the heathen — and even by many Christians. But we should not do so. They should correct it and speak not thus!' (*Enarr. in Ps.* 93). Apart from the 'Lord's Day' Augustine favours the old Jewish number-names, which is still what holds today in the liturgical language of the Catholic Church.*

An extreme example of the struggle against the cosmic day-names is provided by Martín de Brancara, a Spanish bishop of the sixth century. He goes as far as declaring the planetary gods of antiquity to be ordinary and even criminal human beings who in former times lived in Greece. Thus Jupiter was an adulterer, Mars a ruffian, Mercury a thief, Venus a prostitute, Saturn a child-eater. They were *homines pessimi et scelerati in gente Graecorum* (the worst of men and rogues among the people of Greece (*De Corr. Rust.*) This representation is indeed a nadir in the lack of understanding of, or in the determination not to understand, ancient mythology and its pictorial language.

While the resentment in these voices was narrow-minded and restricted, we must also try to understand the opposition by Christianity to the adoption of the planetary names. 'All things are yours', but 'you are Christ's'. If the second sentence loses its force, and the real Christ-element becomes ineffective, then in reaching for 'the treasures of the heathen' one becomes alienated from one's own treasures. If in the sense of the Apocalypse the glory of the nations is to be brought into the heavenly Jerusalem it must undergo a rebirth through the Christian element.

*Portuguese, unlike Spanish, keeps to this practice.

The exalted mystery-wisdom of the ancient Chaldeans had already assumed a very decadent form when it was being spread through all sorts of murky channels in the Roman Empire. Juvenal complains in his satires: 'But there is even greater confidence placed in the Chaldeans. Everything told by the astrologers is taken as valid . . . for now the Oracle at Delphi is silent and mankind is tormented by the darkness of the future' (6:554). Men were made unfree thereby. They held the stars responsible for their own misdeeds. The Church Fathers had to concern themselves at times with such views. Against the turbid after-effects of a once exalted star-wisdom Tatian (AD 170) was assuredly right when he said: 'We Christians stand above fate (*heimarmenēs anōteroi*) and instead of planetary daemoni we have known the one unerring Lord' (*Or. ad Graec.*9). The Christian is 'above the compulsion of destiny': a glorious saying.

Even so the 'all things are yours' remains. Of the sabbath Christ said it 'was made for man, not man for the sabbath, therefore the Son of Man is the lord even of the sabbath' (Mark 2:27f). Man's becoming is the meaning and goal of Creation. Man may not surrender his freedom to what has been created for him. Once his freedom is assured through his attachment to the Christ then he can and ought to avail himself of all that can help him towards his development. In the deepest sense Sunday also exists 'for man' as the 'day which the Lord has made' for the good of mankind. In this sense the Son of Man is also lord of the cosmic forces. On Patmos John sees the Risen One holding the 'seven stars' in his right hand. They are the seven genii, the seven world-qualities. In this connection we can also consider what the seven day-gods were for the Chaldeans. In the decadence of the ancient wisdom a stage was reached whereby man felt himself without freedom 'in the hands of the seven stars'. John sees it the other way round: the seven stars in the hand of the Son of Man. They are subordinated and integrated to his higher working: they must serve him. Under this sign is set the task of future Christianity, that is to bring the cosmic wisdom to a baptism whereby it can be reborn as Christian wisdom. That applies particularly to Sunday, whose Sun-character is confirmed and strengthened by Christ's Resurrection, and which stands ready to be apprehended by Christendom with a new consciousness.

Of that there is little to be seen in the history of the representative churches. From the fifth century onwards in Roman-Greek Christendom the use of the cosmic week day names began to decline. The residue of ancient wisdom was cast out, no effort was made towards its rebirth within the Christian element, no attempt was made to bring it home to the New Jerusalem: a Christianity bereft of wisdom was all that was desired.

A consequence of this was that in the sixth century a 'sabbathization' of Sunday began. Ignatius of Antioch had warned against confounding the sabbath and Sunday, but already the sense for the difference in genius of the two days was lost. There was no longer any feeling for the Saturn character of Saturday and the sun quality of Sunday. And so the mood of the Jewish sabbath began to be implanted on Sunday which was being turned into a Christian sabbath. The scholar of early Christianity, Theodor Zahn, wrote: 'It never occurred to the Christians of the first three centuries to consider Sunday as a continuation of the Jewish sabbath or even to call it the sabbath, and even in the fourth and fifth centuries only uncertain beginnings of such an outlook are to be found'* By the time of Charlemagne the blurring of the difference was in full swing.

The Reformation, having no knowledge of a Christian wisdom, brought no return to the original usage. Here the only consideration was social and educational, and it was decided that there should be a work-free day for religious instruction; and in the interests of good order a special day

*Geschichte des Sonntags, p. 128.

had to be agreed upon. 'Because from former times Sunday has been assigned to this purpose we should leave it at that, that it may continue so in good order by common consent'. (Luther in the Great Catechism). Calvin's Protestantism, bearing the strong imprint of the Old Testament, almost completely transferred the sabbath mood to Sunday. An amusing picture of this puritanical strictness of the sabbath is given by Bismarck in an address to the Reichstag (May 9, 1885), when he tells of his first journey to England in the 1840s: 'I had just landed . . . on a Sunday, and was glad to have survived a bad crossing, so that I was involuntarily whistling a tune, not very loudly, and a fellow-passenger accompanying me said to me rather anxiously: "Please sir, do not whistle". I said, "Why shouldn't I? I'm happy!" "It's Sunday," he explained to me benevolently, and that I was in danger of being exposed to some unpleasantness.'

Nowadays for many people Sunday has become more and more externalized and submerged completely in the idea of the 'weekend'. We have almost completely forgotten that Sunday should not end the week but should be the beginning of the week, shining into it with the power of Christ's Resurrection. Because the 'true' Sunday is threatened by a calendar reform — and also because the movable Easter festival is even more acutely threatened — we should take this as a signal for Christendom to rouse itself and think about its Sunday. We stand now at a time when it is imperative to attain a wisdom and knowledge of the workings of cosmic powers and their intimate rhythms, and this through the 'freedom of a Christian' as Luther rightly puts it, and in the sense of those words 'All things are yours, but you are Christ's'. In Rudolf Steiner's Anthroposophy we see such a modern wisdom, which has as its centre Christ and the Deed of Golgotha.

16. SUNDAY: A CHRISTIAN FACT

Appendix: The week and calendar reforms

We shall now deal expressly with an objection that is often heard. The 'genuineness' of Sunday depends on whether the weeks have flowed without interruption since the first Sunday. Many people believe that this 'genuineness' must have been affected by former calendar reforms.

At the time of Christ the Julian calendar was in force. This had been introduced by Caesar with the help of an Alexandrian scholar in the year 45 BC. In 1582 it was replaced by the calendar of Pope Gregory XIII, because it had become apparent that the Julian Calendar with its 365¼ days was not accurate enough, the year being actually 11¼ minutes less. This discrepancy, small at first, accumulated in the course of centuries until finally it was noticed clearly that the calendar was falling behind the real sun year. In autumn 1582 the calendar was turned back to the position it held at the time of the Council of Nicea (AD 325) by removing ten surplus days from the year. October 4 was followed immediately by October 15. But the course of the weekdays was not affected. October 4 was a Thursday, and the next day, 15, a Friday.★

The order of the days of the week in fact has not been altered since the time of Christ, and even before that it goes back undisturbed to the sixth century BC. This order has remained constant both in the Jewish congregations, who were really practised in preserving their holy times amid whatever calendars might obtain in their surrounding world, and in the Christian Church, which whether it was persecuted or recognized, has held to its Sunday up to now.†

★The adoption of the Gregorian calendar followed later in some countries, for instance in 1752 in England. The Eastern Orthodox Church still uses the Julian calendar.

†There have been temporary interruption, for instance during the French Revolution with its calendar of ten-day 'weeks' which was in force from 1793 to 1805. Similarly after experiments with a five and six day week the Soviet Union returned to the old week in 1940.

Bibliography

Benz, E. *Adam — Der Mythus des Urmenschen*, Barth, Müchen 1955.

Bock, Emil. *Genesis*, Floris, Edinburgh 1983.

——*Moses*, Floris, Edinburgh 1986.

——*Kings and Prophets*, Floris, Edinburgh 1988.

Dölger, F. J. *Sol Salutis*, Münster 1925.

Gorion, Micha Josef bin, *Sagen der Juden*, Frankfurt a.M. 1926.

Kerényi, Károly, *Die Mythologie der Griechen*, Deutsches Taschenbuch, München 1966.

Scholem, G. G. *Major Trends in Jewish Mysticism*, Schocken, New York 1946, and Thames & Hudson, London 1955.

Schürer, E. 'Die siebentägige Woche' *Zeitschrift für neutestamentliche Wissenschaft*, 1905, pp. 1–66.

Steiner, Rudolf, *Christianity as Mystical Fact*, Steiner, London 1972.

Wistinghausen, Kurt, 'Der Brunnen', *Die Christengemeinschaft*, 1931, pp. 167–72.

Zahn, Theodor. *Geschichte des Sonntags, vornehmlich in der alten Kirche*, Hannover 1878.

Index